STRANGE NURSERY

STRANGE NURSERY

New and Selected Poems

Esther Schor

The Sheep Meadow Press
Rhinebeck, New York

Designed by S.M..
Distributed by The University Press of New England.

All inquiries and permission requests should be addressed
to the publisher:

The Sheep Meadow Press
P.O. Box 84
Rhinebeck, NY 12572

Library of Congress Cataloging-in-Publication Data

Schor, Esther H.
 Strange nursery : new and selected poems / Esther Schor.
    p. cm.
 Includes bibliographical references.
 ISBN 978-1-937679-04-0
 I. Title.
 PS3619.C454S77 2012
 811'.6--dc23
                        2012001312

Acknowledgments

American Scholar, "Laika"

The New Yorker, "Üsküdar"

Raritan, "Budapest"

Southwest Review, "Sapere Vedere," "La Rambla"

Vintage, "Ulica Okolnik 2," "Last Bear" (as "Aldenhofpark")

The Yale Review, "Zion"

Kelsey Review, "Fireflies"

National Poetry Competition Winners 1996, "Leap Day"

The Jewish Quarterly, Michigan Quarterly Review, "Opera Without Words"

Michigan Quarterly Review, "Guggenheim Abstract"

Sequoia, "The Works of Galla Placidia," "My tooth broke today"

Judaism, "Alef"

Times Literary Supplement "At Dove Cottage," "Shap Abbey"

The author also wishes to thank John Taylor-Convery and Rosemary Tribulato of Archer Books, original publisher of *The Hills of Holland*.

For

Daniel

Jordy

Susannah

You'd think it would be easy, living.
All you need is a fistful of earth, a boat, a nest, a jail,
A little breath, some drops of blood, and longing.

–Adam Zagajewski (tr. Clare Cavanagh)

TABLE OF CONTENTS

One

Three

Four

THE HILLS OF HOLLAND

III Cumbria

IV The Hills of Holland

One

HARVEST

Rationale for Using Animals.
Rationale for Using Selected Species.
Consideration of Alternatives.

You'll start with fish and housesparrows, move on to fruitbats
and California mice and work your way up to the transgenics
and the NHPs—

NHPs?

—non-human primates

Pain Categories:
        B. No Pain—housing, identification.
                tattoo, ear notching
        C. Pain or Distress of Short Duration.
                radiation, parasites, gavage
        D. Pain or Distress Amenable to Anesthesia.
                burns, cannulation, tumor induction, predator-prey interactions
        E. Pain or Distress without Anesthesia
                lethal dosage studies
                functional deficit (eg paralysis)
                deviations from euthanasia protocols

pretty basic: anesthesia may compromise data and
no, there's no level A

I remember his lab, the cages piled one on another,
the din the door opened   and closed on,
reek of pee, iron, cedar   (I xeroxed my hand,
carried my third hand home)

how the bungalow smelled   in March, when we slept
in parkas on daybeds

The Porsolt Swim Test is a rapid procedure for assessing behavior depression. Rats do not sink for more than a second during periods of immobility, but float almost effortlessly with their heads above the water. Rats tend to give up sooner in successive swim tests.

we say "dams and pups," not families

anyway, rats are natural swimmers

"kids are natural swimmers," she said, only I wasn't
not natural not breathing   not floating
the dead man's
wreath of kelp, mica crown—

now I know when not
to breathe   I swim in chlorine pools
among the creatures of the deep:

latticed spines, sutured thighs, stumps
and withered limbs, flesh streaked and wimpled,
scarred, and burned

since water closes its eyes   takes us all in

3

This is the ritual in cases of jealousy. If any man's wife has gone astray and broken faith with him and there is no witness against her

transgenic mice   quivering, pink, hairless—
immunosuppressed   the thymus
bred out of them

(the souls of mice)

The procedure for implanting cranial windows onto the skull of mice has become fairly routine. Most every mouse fully recovers.

why do I keep   telling you
about the mice

but a fit of jealousy comes over him and he is wrought up about the wife who has defiled herself
or if a fit of jealousy comes over one and he is wrought up about his wife although she has not defiled herself

the hungers
hunger breeds—
a raft of chow
a drip   a gyre

unadmonished wheel

Live decapitation by DECAPICONE ™ is a necessary and standard procedure for obtaining blood for measures of circulating hormones and metabolic fuels.

4

For thoracic surgery, use
things you have
on hand:

Xacto knife, scotch tape, eyelash glue

Brain surgery requires
a dental drill

alka-seltzer (1 per 20L)
euthanizes fish

The experimenter gently holds the rat so that it crawls into the guillotine. The decapitation is done extremely rapidly, thus minimizing any stress to the animal from being held.

pick up a mouse, his little adrenals will just
blow this stuff out

it's a short list, "what could go off at
any moment"—

a bomb
a lover

the man shall bring his wife to the priest. The priest shall bring her forward and have her stand before the LORD.

any sanctuary will do
just don't forget
that I'm your ride

Human subjects are not appropriate for dominance studies. Memory persists between trials. Experience effects are not well defined.

come catbird
come sparrow

Nests, roosts, and hibernacula are all within the survey. With catbirds you can expect temporary anosmia.

into our nets

wherever they are—Nashville, Cabo—
the transmitters fall off
and they're on their own

If the bird seems weak and not willing to fly, "humming bird water" will be administered to the side of the beak.

what frays, what scabs, what's
debrided

and place in her hands the meal offering of remembrance, which is a meal offering of jealousy. And in the priest's hands shall be the water of bitterness that induces the spell.

Raban Gamliel says: Like she did the doings of an animal,
so too her sacrifice is the food of an animal.

"Cave canem"
says the dog in you

And the Cohen grabs her clothes; if they tear, they tear,
if they tatter, they tatter; until her bosom is exposed, and
he undoes her hair. Rabbi Yehudah says: if her bosom is
comely, they do not uncover it; if her hair is comely, they
do not undo it.

like a fighter
pilot   like a Brylcreem
hero   like there was
no tomorrow

death soared

 circled

a holding   pattern.

They said, "she passed"
as if she were an hour

She will not be done drinking until her face turns green and
her eyes protrude and her veins become filled, and they say
"Take her out," so the enclosure does not become defiled.

Here the priest shall administer the curse of adjuration to the woman, "May the LORD make you a
curse and an imprecation among your people, as the LORD causes your thigh to sag, and your belly to
distend; may this water that induces the spell enter your body, causing the belly to distend and the thigh to sag"

As for Patsy   once her hind legs failed

we chose her last hour

she lay just there   as if to say

in your hands   clouds
where her eyes were   and ready,
the soothing vet from Ottowa.

Syringes, questions:
would she have wanted…
what would you want…

And the woman shall say, "Amen, amen"

On what does she say "Amen, amen?" Amen on the curse,
amen on the oath; amen on this man, amen on the other
man, amen that she was not defiled, and if defiled, that he
will come to her.

Once anesthetized, the monkey will be positioned on the surgery table in a sphinx position with the head raised
on soft towels

I said, get with the program:
for a surgical procedure, you need
a surgical plane of anesthesia,
you're not just harvesting organs

this flutter
this moving air,

rachid, barbed,
covert, it is only
your hand

If she was clothed in white - she is clothed in black; if she had ornaments of gold, and chokers, nose rings, or finger rings - they are removed from her, in order to disgrace her. And after this an Egyptian robe is brought and is tied above her breasts

sharp blue corners, tattooed
around the breast for

(once she said) archaeologists

and all who want to see may come to see, because her heart is known to them

Should an animal become fractious every effort will be made to place the animal in a primate sanctuary.

gas is cheap in heaven but look

it can't be easy for them,
not enough
fenders to lean on, candles

all blown out

Each incident is recorded in the Scratch and Bite book.

it's hot, neurogenesis, think
Alzheimer's

stage six:
he admired the man in the mirror, a surprise

visitor, he combed the man's hair

a fire, a clear-cut, a wave

then (surprise) a visitor whose hair
he combed

a downpour, a fig, a surprise
visitor

and you haven't been tested?

Why?

stage seven:
he admired the man in the
mirror, a surprise

10

visitor, he combed the man's hair

no, there's no stage eight

I added sevens (eros)

I subtracted sevens (thanatos)

Refrigerator A: Animal Carcasses for Orchard Hill Crematorium. No food or supplies allowed.
Refrigerator B: Clean Carcasses for Raptor Trust.

Never underestimate a monkey: keep on
the goggles and don't make eye contact

Patrice
Simon
Bradley
Lennon
McCartney
Vanilla Ice
Mojave
Battista
Shaft
Biggie Smalls
Bush

(the mean one's Gandhi—)

whassup guys?

I saw your MRIs:

glades vines fronds
sweet flag
corpus callosum

venous palms
pia, dura
sea salt

wild turmeric

Stress levels will be measured noninvasively through a fecal cortisol assay. "Lake pigments" used to distinguish feces.

Not bad at all: popcorn every afternoon at 4, ice cubes with
a grape inside and all the phone books they can rip apart

Euthanasia must occur within the vivarium. Principal investigator must specify research endpoint.

it means you have an obligation
to verify death

you stare at your feet   at the earth
as if for the first time   so odd

you're in air   she's in dirt
you're plodding around   she can't move, so odd

he's glued to cartoons   gumming a grape
at the bars, odd when he   catches your eye and

you know him   from somewhere,
some older world

A) Approved Methods:

intravenous or intraperitoneal barbiturates
    Decapicone ™
    CO_2 chamber (Slow filling minimizes nasal/ocular irritation. Wait 3-5 minutes. Eyes should be fixed and dilated.
      Consult SOP before use.)
    exsanguination
    cervical dislocation
    immersion in benzocaine (fish and amphibians only)
    (NB: Chloroform is not acceptable.)

Standard Operating Procedure as in, that's just the SOP.

B) Unapproved methods:

(to be completed by principal investigator)

what don't the dead do?
it's a long list

clamber, groom,
dance, mate,
chase, scratch, scamper, growl, bite, bleed, write, gnaw

13

ruminate, chatter, swim
sing, butt, mount, suckle
listen

If the animal is not dead, return it to chamber, recharge and wait 5 minutes. Or use scissors to open chest cavity and create pneumothorax. MAKE SURE THE ANIMAL IS NOT AWAKE WHEN YOU DO THIS.

a log, histology
a spectral lobe

dark to them,
red light

bring on the night

meet
in a tremor

perfuse chambers
of the heart
with bitter water

raise   a blade
cut
take your harvest

in your hand

Two

Üsküdar

All the tulips of Topkapi couldn't get me into bed.
From the *matrimoniale*, you raise a lens

to bare cathedral windows: *See what you
missed? And here's the pilsner took me*

halfway through a life of Atatürk.
A rangy shimmer widens, upward, outward,

a fat girl breaststroking the Bosphorus,
trained for meets. Foothills drowse on bays,

clouds loosening their scarves. They all but touch,
the continents. In the Courtyard of the Favorites,

revisionists with screwdrivers. Daughters born
to scribes and merchants, plucked like snowdrops

from the provinces for—cancel "comeliness and grace"—
discerning intellect. Nine silver-fauceted hammams,

the Chief Consort's carpeted loge for tea with the Valide Sultan,
the Valide Sultan's screened arcade for tea with the Chief Consort,

kiosks for eunuchs, a fruit room for the Prince, a ward
for gravid odalisques. Hence decorum, hence unguided

smoke-free tours. What did my cupped hand prove?
Who made straits this wide? Here nothing's fruitless,

sweet teas chase hard bargains, empty bowls
of pomegranates, peacocks, reeds, and cobalt fish.

And jealous I am, not for a glimpse of Europe
leering at Asia, copping a feel; for sheets unseen,

cries unheard —*O hasten to Allah*—in Üsküdar,
where calls to prayer, do for prayer.

Zion

we call this the clear blue sky
said Edge, who called
his horse Judge, the sky

above all, flawless,
remorseless
blue before the

firmament
flooded the mind
of god, before

transgression
left quaternary
lakes gone to vapor

a million years ago
omens
of what's passed

somehow,
the aquitard,
slickrock

apertures,
a throbbing ocean's
ghost pinks

siltstone basins
at the rim
and heaving, faulted

canyons named for men
named by winged
monuments quarried

in Danby Vermont (since
nothing atones
like stones)—

Alonzo Russell
Killed by Indians,
Electa Badger

a kind mother
a dutiful and affectionate
wife a faithful

saint awaits
a resurrection
with the just.

Souls rise
like dust
from raftered

barns and even
fins and cliffs
ascend to pinnacles.

From Angel's
Point, my pissing
mule adjusts

his sights
downward
close your eyes

on the turns
he don't need
your help so

tempting
to regard
the Virgin River

as a frail
replica
of mighty

waters,
since an eye's
a withered

cataract
a heart's
a windbreak

the mind, a stand
of bristlecones
where trails meet

and part just as
the graveyard shift
at Boulder City

once they'd plugged
the diversions,
broken camp

went their ways
the twenty centers
west to peach groves

in the Imperial Valley
the fifty centers
north to ranches

in the high country
and no one
carrying

into the next life
shovels they called
crutches and banjos.

BUDAPEST

I Szigetvár, 1566

Infidels came to this bridge in midwinter,
speargrass armored in frost. Leaping the river,
the farmers' frantic cries acquired

an antic air. In August, the shabby Turks
returned, sacked the abbey, burned
the barbican: bloom of fire, storm of soot.

Look, said the painter, clouds
foam higher and higher, bruit
blue tears of sky to the soldiers there—

sordid arrows, arrogant swords.
Here, said the painter, a tiny splash
where the last words of Suleiman

sank, his corpse lashed to a chair
carted aloft to meet
the steed of Zrínyi, his prize, his white Arabian,

from whom the victor of Mohács toppled, moments later.

II Aszú

Fingered grapes
pressed of ichor

under their own
weight—

call it essence,
or liquor—

husks crushed
flesh into blood

jewels immersed
a barbarous flood.

Eight summers
in oaken barrels—

a vole's dream
oblivion's lake—

flesh and blood.

III Heroes' Square

The bronze prince, his seven Magyar dukes
and seven Magyar mounts, robed in verdigris.
A century since the millennium, I'm green

with envy. Not for the mud-medaled
chieftains who opened Hungary's veins.
For nurses buying late carnations
by the tram, florid widows damp

from the baths, pigeons cooing their
intricate loves. Arms high above their heads
boys slash the marble concourse

like ancestral swords,
descendants of Arpad, on skateboards.

IV Rigó Jancsi

(violinist, namesake of a favorite Hungarian pastry)

Owls turned when he bowed the E string,
waiters paused. His gypsy violin
carried from one millennium

to the next, capital to capital;
masculine, feminine. Torches flared,
his bursa, inflamed. Klara felt an echo

of his ache, a twinge of *Magyarisme*
in the Bois de Boulogne. Who's to blame her,
platinum to the bone,

Mrs. Count of Caraman-Chimay,
(née Grosse Pointe), a village famed
for cloisters and beer. Children

left with a maid, they rode through the night
to a galloping *verbunkos*
down avenues of plane trees, amid empties

of Dom Perignon, past Cap d'Antibes,
past Monaco, to Székesfehérvár,
where they slummed a week with witches

who read their Tarot—*the Lovers, the Fool
the Ace of Cups*—and on to a cottage
in view of the Nile

where she taught him to read and write.
And after two or three floods,
practiced at kissing goodbye

in the Continental style, she left him
for a man with eyes of *ganache*,
a conductor for the Vesuvian Railway.

V *Szép Ilonka* (Matthias Fountain)

Out of the golden forest, under the pleachèd
branches and dark vines, straddling mottled
boulders, Matthias in royal relief, every inch

a Prince. But so is every man, posed with his kill,
a vanquished stag—the forest's prince—antlers
erect. Rivulets of life leak into crevices,

pool out of sight. *Szép Ilonka*, lovely
Ilonka, crouched in rubble, petting a fawn,
thought him a simple hunter. But every woman's wrong

when a horn held to lips enters her,
ravishing, abrupt, final. Forgive her
the bandit-bitten roads to court,

her slow way home, her festering heart.
Forgive the shaken fawn,
he'll die this way too. Forgive the mastiff

his panting mastery, his tongue lapping the clear stream,
suddenly savoring blood.

VI Radnóti's Pocket

Not a word of German till we reached the camp.
My mother tongue said *march* and *halt*,
put me on this train. My morning bread
is dark. Engines stitch the sky, breath shallows
to a new regime. Farewell, pale moon of Serbia—

beyond this ridge, Bavarian dawn.
Angels make poor sentries.
If I could, I'd live in my mind:
What juicy summer, what wet year? Who passed
this cigarette to me, a carmine kiss? I'd join

the monkey in his gibbering palm,
swinging from line to line in my poem,
scratching his blue ass. *Admit me*
to your academy, let me ponder your dialogues.

This cigarette I kiss, I've made my wife.
Ten poems *shuckle* in my pocket,
in the holy tongue of worms. I'll count on
their lovingkindness
when I'm shot at the dam near Abda.

Ulica Okolnik 2

The conservatory guard
taps a foot, under wisteria
cellists light up.

A flag, a pulse, a curriculum,
twenty-four preludes and fugues,
Copernicus, Curie,
Kazimierz Funk

the father of vitamins,
Poland's five oldest oaks:
Chrobry, Lech, Czech, Rus

and Bartek, near Kielce,
say the schoolgirls, all between
700 and 1000 years old.
Committed to memory,

the words of Zygmunt,
the last Jagiellonian –
"I am King of the people

not judge of their consciences."
Among the holdings
of the Jewish Museum,
the staff of the Rebbe

of Turzysk, carved
in ash, attends
a photograph from the

Bobowa Gazette: four generations
of Chernobyl rebbes
arrive to take the waters.
Their Talmud's

gone, and in its place,
encylopedias of bread:
Stale, it keeps.

It buys warm water.
Snow falls on it,
a taste of sugar.

And for all who arrive
at Umschlagplatz
in a timely manner,
a loaf of spelt, a kilo

of marmalade.
A filmstrip on ghetto
routines: Tuesday mornings,
deportations, Tuesday evenings,

cabaret. Last night
beside the bronze Mermaid
in the Old Town,

(the ancient heart of Warsaw
rebuilt one stone at a time)
a girl not much older
than Sue threw

replicas of fire
so fast a circle
blazed through

my dark heart.
Mermaid, in your city
each stone's
at last in place.

Pull back
your hair, have
a beer, drop by
our hotel. Look

for the sign:
NO CREDIT CARDS
NO ENGLISH
NO LIFT

BREAD OF THE SUN

nunca la vida es nuestra, es de los otros
la vida no es de nadie, todos somos
la vida—pan de sol para los otros,
los otros todos que nosotros somos—
                    —Octavio Paz, Piedra de Sol

I Ballet Folklórico

The insert's in English:
*This they dance
in Chiapas, this
in Jalisco,* click click

clack clack. A whirled
rack of postcards
a dance for every region

for every dance, a man
for every man, a woman
for every woman

a tambourine. I'm sick
of local color
the ruffled plaza's
lanterns, its
strummed smiles.

Give me the dance
of the hunted deer again
point of obsidian
antlers scratching
sand, a twisted

torso, torment.
Nothing to be done:
the finale's begun

petticoats flying
sombreros bouncing
electric sunlight thickly
spread. It's just as you

feared: tinny, shiny
lifelike, if you spent
all your life but
a little change
in your pocket

a couple of
tender coins
incised with snakes
or cadets. *Extravaganza*
just as the insert

promised: a true
waste of color.

II Zona Rosa

On Calle Liverpool, potted palms a mile high, drizzled
nightlife, *GIRLS!* Our menu's in Italian,

which must be a test, like that B-movie where they ask
what you were eating for breakfast when Pearl Harbor was bombed

to find the Japanese spy so we confess, as to a brazen truth by which
we will certainly die at dawn, "somos Americanos." In the night schools

America's in flames. Our bowtied waiter bets the world
will end in English, he's probably right. *Good evening,*

*there is smoke in the hall. The door is warm. Please evacuate
the building.* We order mole hot, perhaps too hot: a fuselage

explodes, doors warm up, towers fill with smoke.
When the *mayordomo* turns his back, the waiter

begs a phrase. What comes to mind is *smoke and mirrors,*
a little something to be taken down.

III Pirates

Before the
courts of justice, west
of the sinking Cathedral,

a demonstration:
hundreds of grassgreen
beetles parked on the plaza,
FUERA PIRATES!

A banner year
for crime:

instead of a cab,
a pirate drives up,
sucks out your cash,
dumps you in
Chapultepec.

You bathe.
You eat.
You sell the flat in Polanco,
buy a ranch in San Antonio, you
become American.

We're already
American, we think it will
happen, today,
to someone else
far from the tiled
monuments.

Windows rolled down
elbows crooked,
pirates sway
through narrow
channels, doubloons

sing in their
pockets—
Besame,
besame mucho—
sails full of
air, cash, kisses.

IV At Monte Albán

Paul Kirchhoff (*Hörste 1900—Mexico City 1972*)

My guidebook,
   dogeared, foxed,
      says *sharp tools used*
    as in the glyphs
of Building J, shaped

like an arrowhead.
   Fractal, fraught
      each perfects
    another's pose—
penis or pennant? chiseled

member? bloody
   gash? Five lines
      a hand, three
    a beard, parabolas
of haunches, elbows,

knees. Not even
   Kirchhoff knew
      who named these
    mutilated captives
Los Danzantes

himself a giver
   of names —
        mesoamerica
   coined at his
typewriter

in the garden
   at Coyoacan,
       and the names
   of the thirty-nine
traits: skull trophies,

ear ornaments,
   silent hairless dogs.
       All night, to the
   blanched whisper
of moths

he pecked out
   Comunismo,
       four stiff columns:
   Cardenas selling
Mexico to oilmen,

Trotsky selling
   out. Hitler revoked
       his passport;
   Roosevelt, his visa;
the Fourth International

banned him: *agent
    provacateur*.
       He took
   to calling himself
El Aleman, his loden coat

cut in Westphalian style
   left in a
      union hall
   in Iztapalapa
(no matter who

wore it, always his own
   German coat),
     his *biergarten*
   Spanish a perpetual
penance. In Cuernavaca

Eiffel's bandstand
   recalled the *trencadis*
    balconies
   of Barcelona,
their potted grapes

that blossomed, fruited,
   burst, and there
      he added to his list
   a zoetrope
of maimed and bleeding

chiefs. When the
   typing stopped
      and pulque flowed
   he saw not
warriors, but bloody

caryatids, an obscene
   kick line
      from old world
   to new. My guidebook
riffs on the ballcourt—

games followed
   by sacrifice of loser
      or winner,
   we can't be sure—
silent on the monument

to Dr. Alfonso Caso
   who hired
      Zapotecs
   by the day
for a kilo of cornmeal

to clear stones
   heavy as men
      in his bronze
   hand, a slim
cigarette.

V Guerrero

The *old road's more scenic* says Pepe, like tattooed Bill
the fish guy on Whalley Avenue who told whoever asked

> "what's the difference between grey sole and lemon sole?"
> *it's fishier.* His black Suburban runs downhill

on a cocktail of Pemex and gravity, weaves
blue threads in the *Guia Roji*, the only atlas of Mexico

> there ever was or likely, will ever be,
> to show, in red, invisible frontiers.

Guerrero's the poorest state in Mexico, he says, before we pass
"Tres Marias," the roadside stand—carport, table, girl swatting flies—

> Pepe calls "Tres Amoebas." *Ten years ago right here,*
> *a thousand tarantulas, thirty, forty minutes*

to cross I have never seen this again he says
and brakes: a knot of boys—not boys at all,

> stand in the road, plaid shirts, dark jeans, straw hats
> holding a placard, **ESCUELA NORMAL**,

tops scissored off the plastic jugs they shove
in Pepe's face. I've tasted it before, when black ice

> flipped the Skylark (arctic white, first car we ever owned)
> before I'd borne anyone into or out of the world,

totaled, hushed, neither eastbound nor westbound,
a bitter, wormwood taste of what's to come,

                coming. The kids don't seem surprised, some instinct
                that sends sheep into fields to sprawl on the very

alfalfa they'll eat tomorrow, makes them
stash their Ipods under their seats, some instinct

                that skipped me. Pepe's locked the doors, *Que tal, Amigos?*
                They're shy, since all they have is knives and once

he throws ten pesos in, ten pesos more. My heart,
or Pepe, floors it, *zopilotes* overhead

                since only the Nahuatl's black enough for vultures
                circling above a bloody uddered heap

and on the shoulder, five yards on, two donkeys'
roadside rendezvous. She's unregarding, bored,

                he's vain, peremptory, thrusting his pistol, cameras
                zooming in and out. *Pull over,* Daniel says, but something's

pulling over us charred clouds as torrents
turn agave into flagellants, black crags

                from a painting of the scholar Tu Fu traveling,
                what matters most, the fishbone all his learning

leans on. They sound so similar—*driving rain,*
driving on. Fog screens what must be

Acapulco Bay, no loss to Pepe, since he's seen
palms and pineapples before, no loss to me

since what I've come to see, I've seen
except this arc of seven colors

reared up as one against the mist,
concave, convex, and complicate.

Achilles at Dien Bien Phu

Brigadier General Christian Marie Ferdinand de la
Croix de Castries (Paris 1902-Paris 1991)

At Saumur, twelve and roseate,
new to the cavalry, escorted to

a coalblack Lipizzaner
bred for the *Chasseurs d'Afrique*

he chose instead an ashen Barb
called Diane de Poitiers,

and as he rode her,
conjured English longbows

at Crécy. Immune to his prestige,
impassive when pricked

twitchy when becalmed,
her charm (all his alone)

a cast of amber in her eye. Add
thirty years: pomaded and moustached,

easy with women, inured
to love, seized by a thumping

Bavarian in the name
of the Third Reich

on the outskirts of Oran,
whipped, kicked, given

(as befit his rank) ample
rations of white bread

while back in France
fathers in cravats bought off

the warmbloods, one by one,
to teach *les jeunes bourgoises*

the fine art of dressage
and only a coffered

salon in the Louvre
where noble, carved Assyrians

their steeds in perfect synchrony,
brandished one another's reins

to show there ever, anywhere,
was such a thing as cavalry.

Add nine years to the day,
at Dien Bien Phu, you'd think

the *parachuistes* let down
by silken filaments

now arced, now slack
might salve the morning's sting—

a *piednoir* much given
to spitting between his boots

who'd called them
les putaines du générale—

he should have known:
to name eight mossy mounds

for Saigon whores
Gabrielle, Eliane, Anne Marie

Dominique, Claudine, Huguette
Isabelle and Beatrice.

What was he thinking?
Not of Navarre's incompetence;

when he'd see Saigon again,
tight plaits tiny Eliane

wore like a crown, her mingled
scent of sex and myosotis.

At dusk, as late to some affair,
came Giap's assault: howitzers

lashed to bicycles heaped
with ammunition, rations, tarps

the airstrip strafed, bamboo aflame,
his American helmet, smoldering. . . .

They took them, one by one
his Beatrice with her

Algerians, his Gabrielle
along with sixty from Dakar,

the sisters from Vientiane,
Anne-Marie and Isabelle, the fifteen

Ivoiriens beneath their
skirts. He's down there, too

bunkered deep in Eliane
you'd think he'd have

a pistol cocked to greet
les termites rouges

but when they come
like Agamemnon's men,

they'll find him buried
in Leconte De L'Isle's

L'Iliade, hard at
some general's dream

of feeding his Briseis
fine white cheese and the honey

of Thessalian bees.

Three

Sapere Vedere

At Camp New Jersey,
ten miles from Basra,
a sergeant tells a reporter
before he left he'd ordered
flowers to land on his girlfriend's desk
first Monday every month.
His buddy snorts, *You must
read a lot of books*.
He shakes his head: *It's just
$35 a month. The things I know about love
are scary*. He knows in his gut
they'll advance tomorrow;
he shaves so the gasmask fits.

    When a poem walked by
    Dickinson froze,
    the top of her head
    came away. *These are the only
    ways I know it.
    Is there any other way?*
    On Keats's wrists,
    blood bounced if a poem
    passed. *Great Spirits*
    he wrote, *give the world another
    heart, and other pulses*.
    (This jumping vein,
    I hold it toward you—
    *that beat, that beat,
    that?*) And when Tom
    spit a leetle blood

he knew all he needed to know:
poetry's vital
or fatal. My mother used to say,
I know it in my marrow—at least
she did before a tumor
cracked a femur.

On a study of a horse's eye
He chalked his motto,
Leonardo:
sapere vedere:
to know how to see
(and mirrored, reversed

vedere sapere,
to see how to know).

When the bombing began, the lines were long
at the Met. Guards yielded
a crowd stormed in
I held my ground
before *A Row of Four Mortars*
Firing into the Courtyard of a Fortification.
Four showers of stones
in blithe eruption—
He was having fun?—
you noticed, not a god
in sight. Each stone
drew an arc in the air
too fine, too taut,
to call spray. He saw
they knew, the stones,
how gunpowder flared

in the barrel, how air parted
before, closed behind.
He drew seams
where air ever after
was likely to tear.
The tracer I saw on the news,
brightened, rose; I couldn't
follow it down.
Stones peppered
the squares below,
not thinking of water,
not thinking
of ever rising again
so hot, so tired, so spent.

                    Mancino, southpaw, lefty:
          Freud wrote to Fleiss,
          "perhaps the most famous
          left-handed individual was Leonardo,
          who is not known to have had
          any love affairs" (Viennese wink)

          who, *all'ebraica*,
          reversed the world

          to see, to know
          the stones, the acrid air
          the four dark mouths

          compare what stones left in the air
          (the stain of an idea) to
          what of air was left in stone
          (a lick of rain).

His alphabet of shadows
slopes both ways.

                    Someone's
rummaging for a compact; we came
for lines, not speculation.
Look here, look hard:
stones jump back
along the same black bow
to hungry mouths

as Atlas slows
the orbit of the earth.
And if a few pinks
close, a womb sucks back
an infant, we have words
for that, too: collateral damage.

I'm taken with what
takes you, *A Copse of Trees*
Seen in Sunlight. In a stand
of cypresses, we forget
annotations, canals,
gravity, tides.
We stare two minutes
at red chalk,
know green better.
In the tv room, Jordy asks
why do bombs turn the night
green? A night vision
camera, I explain, my cadence
perfect, maternal. We stare

at the screen:
a stand of minarets
in crosshairs,
auroras of green.

        When I wanted a theme
        I could get my arms around,
        I chose floods.
        I asked fish
        about salvation and salination,
        how the ark looked
        from below. *Watertight*
        was all they said. On Noah,
        they spilled: *He never looked out*
        his window. In the hippos' straw,
        soused on mead,
        he screwed Shem's wife.
        They asked
        when the flood would end.

Won't be long now.
said the general:
a briefing. The *Times* said
months before
we know the extent
of the damage.
Looted museums, munition dumps,
body counts. Pessoa wrote,
"How vast the field is
and how tiny love"—
what I know about love
is scary. The weatherman's hand
sweeps the map:

ninety there
forty here,
let's do the math:

we're fifty degrees
from what we called

the fertile crescent
in Mrs. Walter's fourth grade class
when I, a know-it-all,
stayed up all night
learning to spell
(parched, in the deserts of bed,
in a quilted tent
by penlight)

Tigris
and Euphrates.

Blackout (1977)

At the New Yorker Theater,
    Effi Briest receives a caller
        in a filmy gown—
no letters yet, no accusations.

Suddenly, marriage! Effi
    scratches a pillar for old paint,
        scans the Prussian
waves. They say a Chinese

is buried there; *you hear the sea*
    all the time, she calls out
        to no one, her only
choices, black (men and boots)

or white (girls and dunes), for white
    read grey. July, they're off
        in a wagon for ices
or waltzes: violins belch, gestures

freeze, quicksilver dwindles
    into dross. A man
        in the third row
(the man I came with)

whispers *powerful,*
    a voice from the booth:
        sorry folks,
we seem to have lost

power. This date needs
    an end, so I say
        "we'll talk" and walk
uptown, alone, up shattered

avenues lit by taillights
    already gliding away,
        everything's
up for grabs, what's going on

what's mine, what's yours,
    what's to become
        of Effi once
Roswitha comes out from the kitchen—

Confections? Confessions!— *a child*
    on the third day
        taken away. A kid's
selling candles for ten bucks, five bucks,

three, TVs and jeans fly
    into apartments, in lots
        once vacant,
drums of fire. At Key Foods

on 96th they're cradling
    packs of meat
        so tenderly Effi
chokes down a tear; *too much*

is too much. A summon
    of sirens, salsa
        hoisted on shoulders
thrums on the median, black girls

in disco shorts, the very girls
    Instetten might have
        asked, who can say
anything new? I could have

told him, listen, the hydrants
    are singing,
        but here is
crestfallen Herr von Briest

in his morning coat
    and pale carnation
        telling my doorman
It's too vast a subject —

and here's his pregnant sigh.

La Rambla

Astride a globe atop a column
precisely where he disembarked
a precious haul of six Caribs

whose dark backs the sisters scrubbed
with boar bristles, whose pale souls
the bishop biscuited and claimed

for Christ, Columbus hails
the funicular, a spider's belly
dangled over stevedores

glutting a ship's dark hold
with *cava*. Whose idea, to string
this filament from Barceloneta

to Montjuic, to tip up to the sky
empty sarcophagi
incised with alephs and acanthus leaves,

reborn as rustic troughs?
Three hundred sixty-four days a year,
when we're not here, parakeets

in cages held aloft by fishing line
taunt ocellated geckos,
vitreous, appalled,

behind each stacked terrarium
a muraled predator.
You've found another way

to be afar, after making the best
of a bad situation and getting on
in years, having kept all options

open, like the errant river
leaving a mudcaked rut of a bed
to Moors who called it *ramla*,

meaning *bed of a seasonal river,*
and never returned, bent
on a life undersea, shimmering,

inconsequent. On Catalunya's flags,
Wilfred the Hairy's four bloody fingers
tell his sons to avenge him, not telling them

how. You've found another way
to stay afloat, like a crescent of lime
in icy claret, laid with your girl

whose death no one thought to avenge,
a way not to hear the cloister geese
hymn the virgin martyr Santa Eulalia,

the white doves hatched from her throat
pecking the ears of men
who tore her flesh with iron hooks,

torched her cornsilk hair, a way to prove
nothing at all, so like these human statues
poised for coins—gilt and kohl-rimmed

Cleopatra, cycling fly, Che in olive drab,
his thrust fist unfatigued—still lives so like
your own, lived hand to mouth,

one flash at a time. Let me
carry you off, in pixels, in a tiny silver box.

Guide for the Perplexed

Since the one god who made the heavens
and the earth, leaves you unperplexed

since the god of love grew tall
in your neighborhood, since by some miracle

your guidance falls to me, let's say
it does what fire does, *melts hardens cooks burns*

bleaches blackens, let's say it *goes returns*
ascends and drops, roils and fades

say, for the sake of argument
it is a body you can open wide,

put out your hand and touch,
if only to be asked

what it might ask of you since
poems make outrageous demands,

like gods and lovers, like
a pelican in the wilderness,

an owl in the desert.

For Lori

Love wasn't in the air or on the table, though

One imagined heading out to steep

Regions or gathering, inside, like a kettle

In its last quiet moment, about to send steam

Into air, to become air, to become ever after a

Silken, rare thing, no many, drawn

From a deep top hat, make it an opera hat

Infused with arias: this satin act, now this, now

Fiery towers, now plain June rain and

There, blessing the end of one day and the start of another

You, beloved of God, beloved of us.

My mother surprised me

dead twenty years,
    in catseye sunglasses,

             smoking a Kent.
                It's fabulous here,

cream soda fountains
    heaps of pastrami

             and tongue. "Your friends
                are dying, their hearts

enlarged, their backbones
    shrunk, Dad's brain

             has gone to salt,
                the towers are down,

we're all in camouflage
    and boots—"

             Now girl of mine, I'm
                dying to know—

what's Google?
        what's Starbucks?

                  She waves
                      a copy of *Life*,

out falls a postcard
        mustard-stained.

                  Never mind that, love,
                      just tell me this:

where do I go online?

July 9th

You wanted me married before you died,

but I was a line that wouldn't scan, my coldwater
life, my latitudes too blurred to count, a *mattress*

on the floor type a man who nailed me said.
Love was complicated, apparently, since my tar beach

looked down on his elms, his wife, his child. Heart
stashed overhead, an organ on ice, I flew standby

from the capitol, circling, delayed. No heroic
measures, sixteen years ago, just a Tuesday

I stopped for coffee and the cashier dissolved
into a stockroom so I've had to picture my father,

familiar with every procedure, two fingers
on your neck as Gideon cradled your head,

a ball he was ready to pass. Yesterday, when Sue
stamped a foot to her NO! your *underlovelies*

rose from the hot, lacy chaos of laundry,
settled on one of the piles, along with your face

before the airbrush swiped your moles,
your herring kiss, a window in Frith Street, skeleton

unencumbered by flesh, the shopgirl who said,
it's ten thousand pounds, they apparently

no longer do them in bone.

Eleanor (1933-1936)

The diary you began
another year, come and gone
saw the child come and go

(come for three years,
go in three days)
held visitors' names

and what the doctor charged
and how you paid him
(seascape, 9 x 12),

the ragged Catskill breeze
implored for rest
and sometimes death,

but not the fierce
fine, corona
of heat or how,

pronounced,
it left her cool
as yellow asters

out of season.

Over waffles, Sue recounts her dream

I dreamed we were in the park
with a bag of birds of every color.
I was letting them fly, one by one,
till the chirping bag got quiet
and when I felt in the bottom
the birds were dead. ·

That's what happens
to the birds on the bottom, I said.

And that's what you said in my dream.

Annisquam

We fed them bowls
        of milk and sugar

in what she called "The Studio"—
        picture window

in full view of the estuary, skylight
        leaking where her easel stood.

We played *Go Fish*, at bedtime
        rolled our dough, told no one

our real clothes lay on our real beds
        in our real rooms.

And standing by the sink,
        I watched him scissor across

the bay, the owner of the place,
        buff scion of governors and admirals

eighty, if a day. Abstracted, expectant,
        unbearably rueful,

I might have been a young, whiskered
        advocate in the last days

of the empire, in a city of eaves
        awaiting an hour with his brother's wife

his treasure, his jewel,
        only no treasure, no jewel,

not his. It seeped in, bitterness,
        unfathomable since I was

blessed with my health and husband and babies,
        everything everyone wants

and when he swam ashore, jabbed
        a finger deep in his ear, I shouted,

Feeling good?
        Good—(he panted)—*No, it's hell,*

hell every morning and why he comes to mind
        so many summers since, so far

from shrill gulls and capes of basalt
        I don't pretend to know any more

than I knew then how to pour
        cold sweet milk

into a cold salt sound.

Four

Hearsay

"In Cyprus they say that mice eat iron."
—pseudo-Aristotle

In Crete they say lakes are bottomless. Proof: a drowning stone makes one sound, not two.

In Maldives a monk has a motor fueled by tears. It also runs on vermouth, but tears are more plentiful.

In Trenton an infant was born tattooed with instructions for smelting tin.

They say in Myanmar the ravens were white until the arrests.

In Vancouver boys sleep on toast till the age of four.

In Kashmir, hopscotch is the last refuge of a scoundrel.

In Circassia, rhinos commence on the upbeat.

In Tlateloco, they say the pit where the bodies fell never filled up. With each murder, the pit deepened.

In Finland, some children are born with braids. They are not the lucky ones.

The bees in Salamanca walk to their work.

In Guangzhou the penis of a groundhog, pulverized, cures melancholy. A killer of groundhogs is castrated but no one has dared.

In Illyria a snake shed its skin, ate it and realized its mistake. Then shed and ate again.

In Kamakura, they say you will turn the page before you will turn to God.

In your mother's house the piano was always there, even before the house was.

In Oaxaca the rain falls up (*pointing*).

A man skipped his own funeral to go to the movies. He stayed for eight days, through sorrow and joy, crime and redemption.

In Whitehall, the prime minister outgrew his allergy to long-life milk.

There was once a lake between East 44th Street and East 49th Street; a dig unearthed harps and garbage.

In Borobudur a child was born clenching stones the mother did not recognize. But *her* mother did.

In Washington the Defense Secretary does the crossword in blood.

They say if one more school is named Washington, Brooklyn will fall into the sea.

In Izmir the Turks waltz in cut time, like penitents.

They say in Belle Harbor, the tide rises twice a day.

In Odessa the water is fine once you get used to it. Before that, you will want to die.

There is a lake so clear you can see in it what you'll never become. Some say it is in Canada (Canadians).

In Scottsdale there was a rain date, but it rained.

In Girona a woman struggled for years to learn to dive but by then there was no more water.

In Nanuet a man shot a pistol and instead of bullets, out came his dreams.

In Scythia a second kiss tastes charred.

They say there is no bridge more beautiful than the Manhattan Bridge. They mean it.

In Alma Ata they salute the flag in Esperanto.

In Perth, there is an academy where commodores teach fellatio and chess. It is that kind of academy.

They say on the death march, their toes froze, then their ears, then their hearts.

A man fell into a pit and lay without food or drink, bitten by scorpions, snakes, and spiders. He called it the happiest time of his life.

In Berlin the Chaconne modulated to B flat, once A major ran out.

When the film is over, the stars go on to other films. The film goes on to other stars.

In Weston there is a golden retriever who takes his leash in his teeth and walks himself. He is popular, understandably.

In Penobscot, a man nursed into adulthood. When his mother lay dying she nursed him for the last time; a social worker drew the curtain.

In Port Arthur, there was no going forward and no going back. So they went forward.

In Bloemfontein they place a hand on the nape of a lover's neck and say, "None of it is true."

Laika

Before we said
you're breaking up

I loved my walkie-talkie's
static song, dialed

placid satellites
where weightless

dogs barking
in Russian sipped

vodka through
barberpoles

while all along
as Malashenkov,

late of the Institute
for Biological Problems

told the BBC
it was only Laika,

a brindled bitch
who strayed all the way

from Nevsky Prospekt
to the brazen steppes

past the Samoyeds
Albina and Mushka

sated and caged
in the simulator, taking

by twos the iron rungs
of the Cosmodrome

driven from earth
prone and chained

pulse unleashed
blood aflame, who

dead in the teeth
of orbit four

rounded the earth
three thousand more

then lit into sky
like a feral star

plumed, blind, newborn.

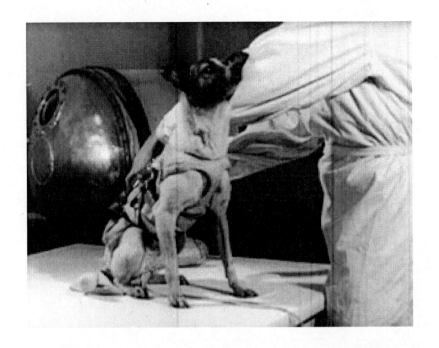

In November 1957, the Russians sent the first living being into space, a three-year old mongrel named Laika. During three weeks of "training," she was exposed to extremes of noise and temperature and confined in progressively smaller cages. With Laika harnessed and chained in place, Sputnik II orbited the earth 2,750 times before disintegrating. In October 2002, Dr. Dmitri Malashenkov revealed that after five to seven hours in flight, the thermostat failed and Laika died.

Missouri

From a stand of bamboo hops
a bluejay

        mottled beak
        bony claws

early, still—
        hoarfrost, moonlight's
        silver spoor—

a rabbit's
paused,

matted, muddied fur.

        If you notice, pocket

a planet

rasp like
spotted frogs

        and ask again:
        What more could anyone want?

(a lookout

             a nosebleed
             seat…)

Smartass:

    say *fir, clause, whore.*

Bluff

    hang onto your jokers

        work at playing dead.

Last Bear

A brewer's guilders   built this circle
of cement where   Aldenhof's last bear—
oh say it—frolicked   behind bars and danced

for dayold bread   collected from cafes.
To set the thing   to rights, a monument
to extinct animals: in fiberglass

a quagga   striped, aghast
dodos bereft of eggs   a Caspian tiger
alert to predators   long dead

a gaunt and prone   giraffe, his neck
arched back   his hooves a delicate
quartet and at his   head, a grieving girl

with wild hair.   She's long on grief—
for the giraffe, for twirling Jo   for erring
centuries.   For us. In bronze

a local sculptor   g's soft as cheese
cast the hulking   form of Jo, as if
sprung from his cage   all he'd desire

was to sit on this   park bench
among the junkies   nappy, pigeon-toed
bent deep in thought   his human hands

gripping the bench,   grasping none of it.

Strange Nursery

—"Aplomado Falcon (*Falco femoralis*),"
Rosamund Purcell

This snowy bed of gauze

      three eggs aligned,
      as magnets to a pole,
      a counterclock of beaks

      ballerinas
      fixed on a point
      in the wings,

      a blizzard of tulle,
      buff and jet,
      candied, cold.

Think: *before you were born,* think

the sofa where she said
you're too crazy
to marry, he said

sleep on it,
and promised to keep
his rifles chained
in a case—

on that sofa, face it,
you'd be out of place,
your arms, your legs:

just so, feather, breast, and claw
belly, neck, and thigh,

just so, bars and bands,
signature moustache.

Heads and eggs: as Beckett said,
a man without a bicycle
is half a man.

Better not to move you.

Stay on your plaid
divan, DVR your favorite
episodes

pretend the incubator's
        a tv, a box
        labeled FLESH AND TOYS.

I've read *A Field Guide*
To the Aplomado. . .

Let's just say, it wasn't pretty:

        yours, the yield
        of smoking fields. . .

        yours, the wolves'
        singed quarry,
        fur and gore.

The twins' father,
dazzled by grace:

Let's not say: *soon darkness will come flooding back.*

Let's say instead
you're cordially invited to
a worry party:

        steam or mist? wet bare night?
        what rate of bleeding is
        acceptable?

             can I save
             this bruise?

That's why we go to bed,
to show our eyes.

That's why it's called the burn ward,
because they set your heart on fire.

Come down, my heart

Come down, my heart,
what do you
see from there?
Here's winter, here's
a ladder.

> *I see the sad angels*
> *five days on,*
> *the eve of Adam,*
> *grey wells*
> *of their eyes*
>
> *snow falling,*
> *falling snow*
>
> *a lighthouse*
> *or an obelisk*
>
> *and your remains—*
> *laddered flesh,*
> *splintered bones.*

This is hard
my heart, I thought
I'd always
have you.

Years I went
by the name
of heart

for fear—
no, certain—

you would turn me out
until the day I found

a window
open, in it

neither glass
nor curtain.

The Hills of Holland

I

Opera Without Words

ANDROMEDA (*The Baleful Head*)

after Burne-Jones

At first light the weird sisters
falcon on the precipices

sharing a picnic of brie and pickle
and under Ethiopian stars, the fickle

Cassiopeia lies in Cepheus' arms.
The briny god concedes her charms

in every glittered wave, and on the strand
toning his biceps, curling granite

Atlas ignores the mackerel sky.
Pegasus kicks in the belly

his *grandes gestes* unsung; shirred
clouds lounge above the leisured

courts inlaid with mother of pearl.
Danaë's an ordinary girl

fair and fey and full of trust
unacquainted with Zeus's lust;

sepia-toned, the Gorgon
tosses writhing plaits, a virgin

learning stitches, doing sums.
Andromeda cocks an ear, runs

a toe against the font—a lute
in the western reaches of the orchard?

Tart breeze at bay, a drizzle
verging on rain, the well quicksilver

and Perseus, oblivious.
Uncoiled, Medusa's

moans attain an acid pitch,
ledges of air in a bruising rush

of shriek and wing. And now he lifts
the lidded prize, and clasps her hand, as if

to say *I can already see the night
your heavenly face shines down*. She might

look away, but without being told,
bends her neck to scan the cold

reservoirs of his achieved desire.
Then what does he see there?

Andromeda, ravished and surprised,
taken by her own green eyes.

HAWTHORNE'S HOPE

You wait but it comes again,
a baby's knuckle, a palsy

a hazelnut shaken from side to side
within the abominable chest

you rest your cheek on the cool
lacquered plank, so close

a feather brushes by—
promise, promise, promise

hereafter, after, after—
and what good is a lid for

but lifting, you say to Epimetheus
who knew you would all along

since he saw you cradle one arm
tenderly in the other, the first time

you touched yourself.
Now Hope's taken wing

it makes a little difference,
cerise wash in the sky, a darker

timbre in his voice, viola
to cello. What to expect,

the caress you craved
all night on your pallet? A bell?

A pear? *a something beautiful
hereafter*. Epimetheus' wounds

swell and weep, so clear
she'll come to grief. Troubles steal

into grey creases of the forest,
hard to make out

among the blades of Egypt grass,
as though Rackham

had scissored the Fates
for the Tanglewood children

to happen upon later
in their quaint woolen stockings

and flowery names—Periwinkle,
Cowslip, Primrose—still too young

for tutoring, for all the other tales.

THE LATE BATHERS

Many little lies create a great truth.
    —Bonnard

The ball of her foot, immersed to a dainty
parenthesis, in a basin you'll tip and drain,
        burden with pestles and whisks,
        on the mackerel tiles

of Le Cannet, beside a clawfoot tub bought
from a hovering Jew, a knifegrinder in Rue du Foin.
        Born Marie, she called herself Marthe
        and *I'll be here awhile* sang in the peach

curve of her cheek, grey eyes scratched in
with a chicken bone; a daub of ochre later.
        And she, so easily pleased—a calico
        hooded in sheets, a mongrel nursing a sop—

threw the marceled curls of Renée into the grate
stabbed at the canvas until ash swirled like water
        back where it came from, desire
        squandered on love. A pumice stone,

a window opened by hand, then olives
silvering, a sagging upholstery of clouds
        rent by a cypress, now Marthe immerses
        a broad flank, a hip. Her breasts rise

as they sink, a range volcanic, lost, while overhead
finches of pleasure gather—flitting blue, skitter
      of gold. Around her neck,
      serenity closes a silver chain.

She opens her eyes, to see yours
closing; closes them to see
      what you will see there afterward.

OPERA WITHOUT WORDS

For Rhea

i

The day he gave her the *get*
the sheytlmacher said *we'll go for blonde*.
In Borough Park, magnolias preened

amid the pigeons' Yiddish
and all the way to Suffern terminal,
an exile from the married land,

she dreamed the tame victrola by her feet
spun madly round the center of its pen,
a black dog hot for its own black scent.

After tea and busperfumed eclairs,
we closed our eyes in unison.
She took a needle to music, like a seam

that was always coming apart: *Grand Themes
of the Great Composers; Opera Without Words.*

ii

I reap, among the cabbage roses of the pillowcase,
the scent of Shanghai Carp, of West Lake Duck
in the rushes: lemon grass to cut the sweet

swimming flesh. Thrifty, rustic,
we made a meal of it, wandering condiments
just out of reach, our five fortunes, illegible.

Each night I lose them this way:
the children go back where they came from,
through a torn screen door a dog shuts

with his nose, bred to leave. Reversed,
they seem to wave us on, their kisses sting.
Reports deceive; never ask *how was school today*

don't say at the easel, what *is* that?
He'll say *Good*; she'll say,
A house. At the scent of clay,

bicycles fretted, dreaming of rust.
Again you'd let it rain,
as though you'd had, all along,

a sure way to tell percale from muslin,
to translate the Norwegian girl's diary
on the day she wrote all about you, because

she failed to say what it was like to dream
in English, to have eaten so many verbs.

iii

We couldn't get over the saucy hip
on Donatello's David; a newborn calf dropped in hay,
blind and pink as a hawthorne. What could not

get over us: creosote in the Star Ferry's wake,
suburban moonlight treading door to door,
evangelical, dopey. The stuff novels are made on,

a neckline lower than low, breasts in relief, a nipple,
scored, fingered. Once again, I become the tongue
in your mouth, what I might say what you might say,

spring rain wiping the desert. And nothing, nothing
beating between your ribs but heart.

iv

In Kowloon, all brides eat beggar's chicken,
and I was no exception. A cake in tiers,
raspberries shipped from Macao. As long as you

threw confetti in lieu of rice, as long as you signed
right to left, it took. After their day jobs,
before their night jobs, boys in dragon boats

strewed the harbor with pistachios,
drumming to combinations of waves.

V

Chelm had its theories, and Warsaw:
you hear one ear at a time—
but only the sound of your ears;

the moon is a slice of cake—
the moon is a butter knife.
What we had to know, we learned,

the way hitchhikers from Montreal
in the absence of priests and maps
learn somewhere west of Tulsa

to spend afternoons at the Safeway
among aisles of frozen orange juice.

vi

From a virgin, the oldest question:
Can a tampon get lost inside my body?
Next month she'll ask again, as though

the circular were code, as though jewelweed
weren't the remedy. A cramp in the last leg
of our journey. As we finally master our cameras,

what claims our admiration?
Modest capitols, decorous ads:
cars for prawns, ovaries for men.

On the backs of bridges and towers, you write
in white space: *I am at home here. No here. No here.*
When learning the beards on national stamps,

kindly refer to your guides: *Florilège, Keepsake, Brown's
Compendium of Deer.* The thirsty waves, the tragic drums,
arias of salt. The token says (if you hold up your change

to the light, if you read Chinese):
The Last Nickel Ride in the World.

GUGGENHEIM ABSTRACT

Tell me your story, the turpentine said:
introduce yourself,
gesture,
do one of us in. The mayflies' whine,

the rasp of toads, spores peppering
invisibly, the turf; my *once again*
became
this time. How tenderly the red sun sank,

how the moon swiped at the droplets. A man
just left of Frank Lloyd Wright said
travertine,
one finger on *reverse.* The tape loops back

to a plenary address, conventioneers
in velvet galleries. Our work's in progress:
in the beginning,
Kandinsky, and after, Malevich, and then, and then….

What terrible ends they kept from us, singed dolls,
argosies of smoke,
moraines;
and such flat feet, such sexy afternoons in small, Saigon

hotels: *Le Vendôme, Les Quatre Chats.* Weather, slightly foxed—
a drizzle loiters at the corner, blued;
neat Piet
cruises his mind. Now we near the hanging gardens,

give or take a story, what was forest clears,
and in airless elevators, icons shatter
to the hum
of fans. It's before we know any better, the hour

of garters, nylons, menthols, permanents,
in lieu of pockets, welts, an alligator
clutch.
I'll take grey before black, and wait

till Kelley's greens have drained a bottle of chartreuse.
After twelve suspicious fires, they renamed paper
ash.
The Italian girl in platforms gapes—

Millecentonovantasei!—a skull
sprung from Yorick, dipped entirely in pitch,
minutes
of the shadow cabinet. Ryman's still

unravished brides await their picture
grooms who sail tonight from Crete for
dowries
stained with ouzo. Two shades deeper than Macon

a Rothko falls in rectangle love;
you heard me right, my dear, you saw that it was
good.
The day before he died, Zero Mostel stood

where a nippled fruitwood breast gleamed
under the high hats, while several
bushy
thoughts bounced down the ramp into a checker

cab en route to Ozone Park, but that's another story.

LA SFORZA

Lucantonio Cupani, her priest
biographer, parades
Caterina's penances:
maceration, naps on stone,
fasts to quicken

a Sienese namesake
who gave up wine, bread,
water, finally
the cherished turnip—
martyrdom's gorgeous

austerities.
The vellum riddled
with La Sforza's recipes is gone;
a copy rendered
in demure, clerical script

offers cures to the infirm
or simply curious,
since curiosity's
a type of infirmity
as Thomas Trollope knew,

his talismanic quill
seduced by Levantine
mummies, Cornish ghosts,
second-sighted
Turks. Afternoons,

he'd take a good cigar,
a beaker of milk,
back to the study
on a floor too lofty
for the rank *malaria*

and write, sip, puff;
after Neufchâtel
(Rousseau's
faux Grasmere),
in lieu of milk,

a bowl of heavy cream
with a grassy tinge.
"To drive a pallor
from the face: shredded
myrrh steeped a day

in muscat wine,
guarantees carnations
in the cheek." Orangewater
for blotches on the neck,
a remedy to whiten

teeth, and one to redden
gums. One, near the end,
"for multiplying silver"
as though Madama
aped the Jew she'd lured

from Bologna's ghetto—
how, Tom Trollope
barely surmised—to do
the Forlivesi's "little bills,"
douse St. Peter's silver

till it bloomed.

HORACE

Horace, I read somewhere, taught Latin Greek,
taught it to sing. Horace put Latin
out of step, put Latin out

like a hound for the night, till it bayed
at a crust of moon, and sniffed
the air for brine, where it learned

how we ply the dark
from the provinces back to the isles.

THE WORKS OF GALLA PLACIDIA

Late June, the sister of Honorius would rage
against the solstice: *Day worn on a bias,*
impossible to anchor with the fibula.
Trying, I have more than once drawn blood.

Midsummer, she was more composed; *the moon*
sang softly on a bed of wheat. Their sordid secret
strained them, yet they never gave it up.
In autumn, when *Jupiter cast stars into the sea*

like pearls, Honorius moved the court
from Rome to Puglia. She didn't balk;
hadn't he promised her
an alabaster table, porphyry floors,
thirteen-hour lamps? She liked
their privacy, and planned to start
a longish piece on Pliny's verse.

But like all homeowners, she was beset
with mice and leaks; *Scirocco thrummed*
the awnings, sun baked
her brain. She piled quarterlies
on the onyx mantlepiece and left
a life of Hecate
on a low divan, unread.

One made one's choices, in the end,
depending on one's taste in genre.
In the *History* she never wrote,
Empires fell like light.

II

Fireflies

FIREFLIES

You see them by not looking: damp sparks
in the grass, cool glitters
in the elms. Even Patsy
noses the air upward, rising, arcing
gone. This morning, in the library,

A Child's Book of Insects:
First flash, males,
how often says how dire; then females,
how soon after
says everything else—

all preferences known
in a flash: who's who,
who will, who won't,
what will or won't work
out. The Chinese ate them for longevity,

but they're above eating, their business,
knowing when to disappear.
Bitter, but frogs gorge
and gleam. Last night
unmoored a dream of you

afloat in the Dead Sea
reading an aura of
newspaper. I ask what rhymes
with *sand, moon, tears*
you say my name, name, name.

What glows in the ocean?
Sand? Moon? Tears?
That sound you hear,
what you thought were waves,
my name, cresting on rhyme,

cresting on dream. Late
fireflies flare at the hedge,
drop from sight. At your house
all night the roses bloom,
a white the beginning of light.

PUNCHLINES

Netted, aquiver, citronella's all we remember
the sun by, now night pools in the air. A handful

of patio days till he's a Sunday call,
all running heads. No nuns roll downstairs,

no one asks *who's there* when we
knock-knock. In the mind's parade,

orphaned punchlines shuffle and strut:
crosseyed priests believe in Dog

poodles read torah, rabbis eat ham,
fringed epaulets, a dazzle of trombones.

Ten summers ago in Maine,
the platinum lake gave nothing away,

shallow and deep all one, he'd leap
from wherever he stood, out

of his depth, our fault—we found differences
hard to explain. On fingered waves, his name

skipped like a stone. He's Freud's little pauper
still, a holdout for salmon and mayonnaise.

And as you turn the volume down (*Marcel,*
said the farmer's wife, *voici un homme*),

the mailman slips out the door, tasselled, fezzed—
"you told me to fuck him for Christmas!"—

and just tonight, the sky's an old shag carpet
taken up to show the spangled taste of gods

who've since moved on. Scolded, consoled,
Susannah's back (she followed a rabbit

into a neighbor's pines) and turns it up;
she likes it loud and towel-hulas

to the crickets' beat. Tell me a joke
that's not on us. Sue yells to a saltine moon,

the sky walks into a bar! We laugh
as August spits into autumn's eye.

HAYAKUTAKE

For Daniel

This frozen clump of grit, mantled, sunbound, plays a little havoc
with the clouds, the tail of its travels vague, offhand. The epics all agree:
to damage heaven takes more
than malice. At one am his silly
cock a doodle do alarm

earned watering a neighbor's cryptomeria, gives out a crow
and crows again; he yawns, zips up, *jeune perdu*
back in the suburbs, stubbled,
flushed. Between his teeth,
a second dark's inside.

He punches the sky, *you measure like this*, his fist no bigger than a plum
and we exchange a glance, our toppled empire's currency—
don't leave him alone with the stars
to unbuckle Orion's belt,
dishevel the Pleiades.

What Adrienne carried, Park Slope to Torcello, in an oatmeal box
taped shut and magic markered *BONE MEAL SUPPLEMENT*
just as Henry had requested
dissolved in Italian water.
So much for smiling Quaker

subterfuge; she loosened the top and out they swirled
in breezy ashen arias. Venetian monks took meteors for the return
of all agglomerated sin
to earth; it's nothing
you bump to the end of,

sin, it's coda on coda on coda. But there, between what dissolves and what's opaque,
the souls of boys and comets meet, eye to tail, self to shadow, substance to accident.
I know this about secrets:
whatever scatters, matters.
I'll tell him then,

ten years from now, when he takes the whitest sheets in the house,
balls up his shirts and jeans and specimens of quartz
a box or two of reeds,
postcards of resorts. When we close our eyes

the speed of light slows to precisely the speed of darkness.

LEAP DAY: FEBRUARY 29, 1996

For Sally and Joe

Bonus twin, midnight born,
    thirteenth roll in the baker's dozen,
        a day for sambas in the nursing homes—

last dance, ladies' choice! My grandmother
    picked husbands like honeydews
        in the Safeway, where you smelled dung

in the meat aisle, chickens among eggs;
    in sawdust, the footprints of shoppers already home,
        scraping a carrot, boning a fish.

Once a century, it slips through our fingers; next time
    we'll know it was earned, like the seasonal love
        of a neighbor. The other years—

missing? misplaced?—overdue checkup, book drawing fines,
    forgotten lesson. *Today I'll grow extra*
        said Jordy, measured against the fridge before school

and after, *a definite quarter inch taller!*, which I'd gladly give
    to his stunted cousin, two years sick;
        and to Michael, who can't say I want

the day's extra words; and these round hours—
    half to his friend with leukemia, half to mine with AIDS.
        February, a fever you said in Latin class,

while out the window—spring? snowdrop?
    winter? snow? By a shade,
        more is less than enough, but today

after years of scares and tries, Beth had a fine baby girl
    (*She'll have her days and nights mixed up for weeks*),
        a tiny cry an inch from the phone. And afterward,

I hung up a Japanese scroll
    to set something lucky between us
        and what might yet come between us:

six white cranes leap
    into a golden sky.

ALEF

For Robbie

Sunday, far north
  the broad air
leafless, farmstands
  hunch at the roadside
boarded, murmur
  a *brucha* for last fruits—
last pumpkin, last apple,
  last week;
the chill Sabbath
  kept at bay
returns to the schoolroom.
  A moment before learning
what do we remember?
  lamed, a lamp
mem, a mouth
  taf, a table, a tack
as though all letters
  bloomed into things
as though God were wandering
  the vineyard, blessing
the heavy vines. But God's become
  forgetful, we've all noticed
the change; frost cracks
  the folding husks
binds the soil
  where we planted
marigolds; my daughter paints
  in crimson streaks

alef, akimbo, unimaged:
  it says nothing
because the sound it says
  is invisible

TWO FOODS I HATE

Chisel, balloon, osprey
Ode, curio, foolscap, parch
Busker, mutiny, seawrack, quire
January, March.

Slipper, purse, davenport
Timber, mosaic, predella, hussy
Savannah, barbican, fraction, spine
St. Simeon, St. Lucy.

Boneyard, whelp, repeater
Vise, tooth, crêpe de chine
Son of a bitch, mother of pearl—
Limes and lima beans.

SO FAR

Not two inches long, barely grey
the mouse I found lying midcarpet, still
and unaroused. Not normal,
I thought, taking its tail the way

I'd seen a landlord do, using
only two fingers; I was a student.
Accident? Incident?
Call it a finding, a losing.

Not grey at all, a tiny ear
pink, nearly, a pale petal
before you see it, a matter settled
before it matters. Almost clear

of import, weightless. You told me
mice stick madly to perimeters,
one panic after another
and said *sick, maybe*

newborn? What sent it from margin
to middle, it won't tell
and I, born forty years ago, and well
am left to imagine

some longing fiercer than my own
in a far gentler thing.

FIRST SNOW

For Sandra

I dressed you for summer: white linen suit,
tangerine blouse, scarf of silken mint—
sherbet colors, you'd have said,
a good choice for forever

What was I thinking? gulls
scritching, moaning,
on the humid verandas
of eternity

you, on a chaise longue
sipping iced coffee under star palms
splayed fingers
between your eyes and the sun

putting up with the prayers,
the lid, dirt falling stone by stone,
then home again, rested—
tea, boiled eggs, cake.

I say *first* again,
I purse my lips. Snow
shows me my errands,
I'm beyond doubt.

False teeth, false breast
Etruscan replicas
a lock of my hair
bones and baubles gone to ice—

once, I couldn't think your death would last.

THE SNOW GHOSTS

For Daniel, Jordy, Susannah

Where the rise slopes into brambles,
you can make them out:
girls in pink hats coming down,
knees tucked into roasting pans,
boys in balaclavas
on flying saucers. Here before us,
when our architect was a kid
drawing planes, when maples
strode to the ridge. We took half a hill
to house our boys, now swallows
build dwellings
out of ours, they nest
in concrete crumbs.
Something more than a bird
wants back whatever we took.

A man who knew
said *your trees are distressed,*
their crotches are weak.
We thought the woods
would settle us. Deer come
to the glass, tawny,
skittish, whatever
they seek must still be here;
one limps, another
lags, as though

fear were too hard
to remember, after all this time.
Easier to lap at the brook
where the ice gapes,
where you still hear water.

In snowpants, the boys could pass
for trees, thick, dark,
unyielding; *not deep enough*
they yell, as though
the cost of joy were gravity.
How much more can they take
than we can give?

The snow ghosts wave
from the rise
fall onto their sleds, whoosh
through the house; for them,
it's always deep enough.
That chill down your back
as you flip the eggs,
your neck stiffening
over the paper, they go

right through you

thread between the trees
like something blown down, down
from somewhere clear out of sight,
and clearing all the flood lines,
ten years, fifty, five hundred.

III

Cumbria

For Walter and Ray

i. AT DOVE COTTAGE

The morning after we bombed Hiroshima
Helen Darbishire awoke in Sussex
convinced by a nightmare Dove Cottage
would be the Japanese ground zero

as if Rydal Mount, its terraced
greenery cascading over Rydal Water
and field of daffodils planted for a daughter
by the churchyard, buttery and blessed

were but a late surmise, and one returned
before the end to weatherbeaten, timbered
walls and narrow panes, to chambered
intimacy coveted and spurned,

far from an eminence. William's idea,
a passage from garden to study, to avoid
a sooty parlor where Coleridge tried
dipping Schlegel into English tea.

Still in the larder, a page of the Gazette—
a young man of excellent qualities
seeks a position for the summer holidays;
still in the cabinet, Dorothy's blunt skates,

John's dull razor; still before the embers
a whiff of wet fur off Scott's springer spaniels,
thirty-seven shivering animals
sharing three names like a bowlful of custard:

Ginger, Pepper, Mustard.

ii. SHAP ABBEY

The Abbott of Furness sold out to the crown
not so the Abbott of Shap; nothing spared
but an arm of transept, a backbone
of cloister, a tower's shin. Through arches
a glimpse of boys playing bowls, laundry aired
in the dappled shadow of larches.

Two miles away, in the Bampton road,
the tiny chapel of Keld, raftered
and thatched, a thousand years old.
A leaflet given out at mass:
"Can YOU recognize a solvent sniffer?
Is YOUR child using drugs?"

It's after the ravage, plunder, swagging
the armfuls of lead and limestone
carried by torchlight to wagons,
harnesses barely holding the horses,
terrible bells taking the sky down,
saints lying in pieces—

too late for lauds and tierce and prime,
for scathing lanterns shone in the eyes
of urchins bedded on straw and stone.
King Stephen's nineteen winters,
the Abbot of Shap couldn't forgive
(*one leaves through the portal one enters*)

but when kindling blazed and the mead purled
he was known to say: *King Edward lived
like an angel amid the squalor of the world.*

iii. HELEN ON BUSTER

Helen up from Suffolk in her Mini:
"The mother, you see, the mother was Bluebell
so all the calves were named with B's—

Brownie, Bonnie, Bert. Now Buster
was more like a pet, he came, let's see,
the spring of '93. What a scene when Bluebell ran

from the AI man, he fetched her down
at the piggery; nice, he was
but fit to be tied, and the pigs

squealed for hours. The boys,
well Nicholas, gave him his feeds
looked after him, groomed him

with the dog's brush. Had games with him—
got rough, I gave them what for, they still remember.
When he turned two, just this March

we sent him off to a man near Darley
down the A31, who sent him back
in steaks and mince. *And was he tasty! and tender!*"

iv. THE RUSSIAN CIRCUS AT KENDAL

Honking a Porsche, goggle-eyed Ramon
throws nuts and kisses to the crowd. Nitka's
tugged the door off, grinning, boombox hoisted
as the ringmaster—NO NOISE!—unplugs it.
Ramon drives slow enough to drown
a thimble of sorrow in shoesful of vodka.

Cadence of trumpets—interval. Selling floss
the girl who balanced fifteen crystal goblets
on a fingertip counts pounds and pence.
Her acne's bad; after feathers, sequins
and mascara, something's lost.
A lion tamer sells us raffle tickets.

Finale: Galinova and Konrad, so familiar
from the poster, riding stallions bareback
curve on curve around the ring
dressed as Huns, perhaps, or Tartars.
Whipcrack, and two brilliant flags unfurl:
Mother Russia, Union Jack—

a real crowd pleaser, and a megaphone
implores, *Come back and bring your friends!*
We shuffle off to the rented car,
interlopers and itinerants,
here just long enough to know
a bargain at two quid a head.

v. "MY TOOTH BROKE TODAY.
THEY WILL SOON BE GONE."

—Dorothy Wordsworth
Grasmere Journals, May 31, 1802

One hazel nut intended for your pie
would not be mashed.

At tea you served yourself,
after William, after Coleridge,

the third wedge of pie
the fourth slice of a knife

then, musing on the substance
of the word *nutmeat*, you bit

and broke in two the tooth
gone grey and dead in Somerset,

that looked back from the mirror
like a woman smaller and older than you.

As voices rose into steam
you fingered the fragment from your mouth,

and set it on the saucer's rim
like a mirror laid face down.

vi HELEN ON DOUG

Helen in the garden, over tea:
"Just a word now, really; *husband*
Nothing between us anymore,

not for years. Those days in art school,
another world, always ink on his hands;
I'd scrub them nights with Lava

but he left fingerprints everywhere.
Camberwell, it went downhill;
back past ten on his motorbike

knackered, a look at the paper,
and off to bed. Even the pre-eclampsia,
took no notice, what you'd call

a workaholic. Never drank,
him, not one for the pub
(oh, in the country, the occasional crawl)—

they adored him at Time-Life.
But going freelance, and up to Suffolk,
his bloody mother's bloody house,

one bad idea after another. The boys, don't ask;
he'll promise a day at Safari Park, end up
phoning from Milan.

Come Nigel's birthday, I took them down;
lions came up to the window,
they barely noticed, and all the way home

it never came up. (No big cheese,
lions, when dad's forgot
again.)
                    Well, here's to absent friends.

Once they gave me the sack
at the *Weekly*, I stood for the Council—
you know the rest. Paid work

after a fashion; thankgod they compensate
mileage, running hither and yon
three nights a week

up late over zoning reports
up early cooking them breakfast, eggs
and sausage and toast.

Mind you, I'd leave him if somebody came along;
where it went, I don't know
but once it goes, it's gone."

vii. EDINBURGH: THE SCOTTISH NATIONAL WAR MEMORIAL

Just beyond the Castle barracks, cobbles
round a parapet commanding views
east to Holyrood and black St. Giles;
north, Scott's spindle looks about to topple.
Inside the apse, a granite frieze of thistle,
the Highlanders' *Sans Peur* and the Royal Navy
cenotaph: *They have no other grave than the sea.*
A bust of Captain MacConnachie, killed by a missile

at Ypres, hushes the boom of the one o'clock gun.
You'd leave but for the names: Dardanelles, Loos,
Gallipoli, Gibraltar, Palestine,
Struma, Persia, Mesopotamia, Marne.
Below crossed swords, draped in Lancer tartan,
a chill so sharp it cuts July in two.

viii. SCOUT SCAR

Before we came, it had already healed:
north to south three miles long;
below the ridge, a bleachéd field,

rubble fences licked by a tongue
of the Irish Sea, the Morecambe Sands.
Daniel complains about the sun

moans for the jug of ribena, hands
me his camera—"Take me at the edge!"
I've had enough of his demands

of his boyish poise on this rocky ledge,
warn him back to the path
as if to say this limestone wedge

is, after all, a scar, a swath
of earth risen up to the sky
to tell the news about death,

how it comes and goes, how a cry
becomes speech, turns to a whisper.
Not a relic of pain gone tough and dry—

a circular stain left by a visitor.
The jagged scar on Daniel's face
became what he said, as much as his lisp or

even his cockeyed tooth; *nowhere I'm safe,*
not even with you. Like the surgical curve
on my mother's breast, or the crescent I trace

on your back, they unswerve
in the mind, stay straight
as a biblical plot: God loses his nerve

before Abraham. From this height,
you'd think all scars belong to the earth,
each a map that reads us north

and south: *you were already here,*
you have passed this place.

IV

The Hills of Holland

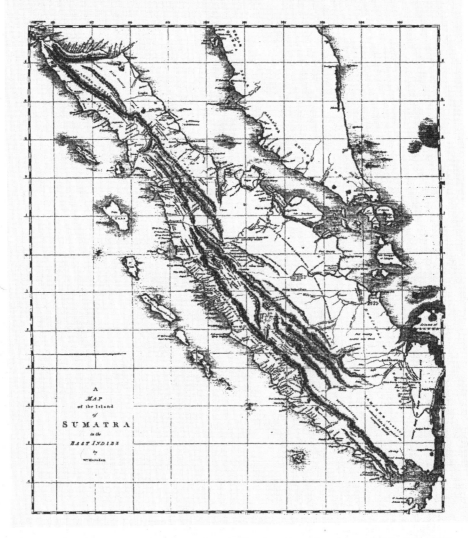

A Map of the Island of Sumatra in the East Indies by Wm. Marsden, published in 1810.

i. William Marsden, Aldenham, Herts.
November 1835.

They have no theory of the scale. My ear
discerns six whole tones, frequent
flatted thirds (*vide* Bengal ragas,
Galway airs), decisive preference
for the minor key.
                      Malay, all vowels
and liquids, makes a music of its own,
Mandeville *Italian of the east,*
ripe to verse's touch. At *bimbang*,
boys of nine or ten extemporise
for hours, legends unspooled
to proverbs' knots. Their choicest form
is called *pantun* (when brief),
or else *dendang*, an undulating
phrasal rush the ear
takes back a moment, till it ebbs away.
Peculiarly, it quits just as it starts.
One night I gave Wasub, God rest his soul,
a pantun of my own—Dyer's *Grongar Hill*
rendered in Malay; it might have been
a Welshman's scorn upon his face,
and *katta katta saja*, all he ventured—
chicken-chatter.
                    They write on paper,
rude pens honed from anau twigs,
characters furnished by the Saracens,
words for butter, milk, and musket borrowed
from the Portuguese.

ii. Nakhoda 'La-uddin, Bantam House, Royal Crescent, Bath. April-June 1829.

In the Name of God, the Compassionate, the Merciful.

To the honor of Nakhoda Muda,
beloved father, beloved son of Nakhoda Makuta, born on Banjar isle
under the Sultan of Bantam, may Allah preserve his memory!
Who made the seven heavens and the earth,

who fashions us from clots of blood
splits the seed and the fruit-stone, and in whose praise
I tell my father's story, the child Tayan and the lordly Kei Damang,
the man who shed names

like a gecko. My grandfather lay
in life's shallows, his voice a chip of shale: "Praise Allah
and avoid to contract debts. If a man greets you,
let your greeting be better than his.

Cut timber, fish, dry more pepper plants
than Sultan needs. Owe nought except to Allah, who winds up the sun
that will outrun the clocks."A dusty voice, he blessed the Day
when men shall walk in broken bands

to be shown their labours.

Honour the mothers who bore you: Radin, O daughter of Paduka,
a dream of copper shoulders, teeth white as tanjong petals.
By *semando*, Tayan married Radin Mantri,

a simple fee of twenty Spanish dollars
and a buffalo. Each night she dreamed the orchards of her childhood,
the cashew-apples of the monkey-jambu trees
woke to the taste of tears

until her womb foreswore its fruit.
And by the second waning moon, she and my father
followed her yearning heart back to the bay
of melons: Samangka.

And from this wife came four,
two daughters and two sons, Wasub and 'La-uddin;
and from the concubines in Bantam, two sons more—
abandoned, disowned.

The bamboo house
swayed and creaked, a vast cradle rocked by trees.
He built the ladders strong; by night four children clambered up.
Between the births

of my two sisters, hill-troubles. All knew
the Abungs' customs: a skull for the father of the bride
full of gold and silver beads, a skin of arrack drunk
to good fortune and good hunt.

I saw my uncle's headless corpse
veiled by white ants, devoured before the evening
rice had boiled. Nakhoda Muda

called a Council of War,
five days the local *pangerans* gorged
on upland boar and dainties, bemoaned a lack
of knives. Till sampans arrived

barely afloat, piled high
with Spanish muskets from the Sultan of Bantam.
At dusk, amid treefrogs' piping and the plovers' pips
the first report was heard—

the Abungs fled, but not before
Nakhoda Muda's anger flared among their fields.
Cassowary birds, maddened by the mingled scent
of sulfur and the flaming camphor pits

shrieked fire-fear till dawn.

My child's-eye met burns and blisters up and down
my father's legs; to reedy sulins and the beaten gong
of victory, they filled and wept.

iii.

Your entry in the *DNB* yields names and titles,
  titles, names: William Hunter Marsden,
      born at Verval, County Wicklow (quite

by accident; your father, having burst
  a fortune in the Bubble, quit Lincoln's
      green unpleasant land and sailed for Cork,

a week on Irish suds).
  Secretary of the Admiralty (retired),
      Past Treasurer of the Royal Society

and Fellow, Asiatic Society, Calcutta;
  Past President, Society of Antiquaries
      (1819, when Graham succumbed

to cholera en route to Istanbul);
  Recording Secretary, Literary Club
      and Honorary DCL, Oxon, a happy

culmination for a Balliol boy
  who, Cicero-stricken, found himself
      on Boxing Day of '79 at Gravesend,

stowedaway on board the *Ranelagh*
  and Java-bound. And made Malay
      his Latin and his Greek.

Close the book; I seem to see you now,
   rolling a currant between thumb and palm,
      firm, unripe, eager for spring

while the unpartnered hand,
   the one you've lost the use of, dreams
      the blushing nuzzle of a rambutan.

Here's shade enough for midday
   scribbling, gravelled walks circuitous and broad;
      with so much said, perhaps one yearns

to say a simpler thing before the end,
   how schist blinked up and down
      the eastern face of Mount Ophir, how light

came through the amber berries of the pepper plants.

iv. Marsden

My *History* (which in its third edition
I consult) begins with vulgar errors:
atrocious customs meat and drink
to them, the old adventurers,
the Polos, Pigafettas, Mandevilles,
cannibals who on behalf of the
infirm, made choice of lesser torments:
suffocation, *then* a stew. To Ptolemy
a paltry Java-bis, or as he put it, *Java-dib*;
to Javanese, *Indalas*; to the Saracens,
who cast ashore Mahomet and his steed,
Al-Rami or *Lameri*; then (and here's
the boxing ring of etymology—
in this corner, Malay *semut*
a large and scrappy ant, and opposite,
samatra, legendary Spanish squall)—
and then, Sumoltra, Samotra, Zamatra,
Samana, and in time, to all, *Samangka*.

v. 'La-uddin

Enter your dwellings by their doors
and fear God, so may you prosper. And from each sleeve
of Kiria Minjan, the Royal Emissary, hung a silken dragon.
With iron claws, they bent my father

to the Sultan's will, to judge
among breathing men. Radin swept between the sago trees,
and there Tayan heard petty squabbles of the pangerans.
Hours baked and crumbled

into dusk, shade pooled
and took him where the voices barely reached. When kunangs flecked the leaves
with sparkles nibbled from the sun, he praised *the fire whose fuel is men and stones,*
spoke judgment and was done.

On a cold, damp isle, where old men
drink babies' milk, I learned a word for my father's gift,
what the English call their game of Sultans and Sultanas
robed in sleeves of darkness

and blood: *patience.*

vi.

A series of authenticated facts
   you undertook to gather and record,
      eight years, thirty-seven days of life

riven into halves of darkness and of light
   by the equator; the ancients built a village
      on the Line, better to beckon

a capable god. Travel five degrees
   northward, land runs out; and south,
      the same, a perfect palindrome,

but for a handful of minutes. *Hence*
   the obscure predilections
      of the surf. It surges in inverse

proportion to the wind, attributed
   to inertia of waters equatorial,
      produced by the increased velocity

with which they spin, which mitigates
   a small, perceptible degree
      of gravitation. From land

you see the swells afloat
   upon their backs, the lifting,
      slender arms of foam draw on the softest

of horizons, varied as the shapes
    the fog assumes; you might be idle Hamlet
        stabbing at the air, but here, amid

the fetid dung of elephants, you glimpse
    a foal, a terrier, the plump cheek
        of a Wicklow girl who'd sailed for France.

Hence, waterspouts that clear a treble
    range of mountains, leeward to windward;
        hence, a swathe of havoc sharper than an axe.

That island to the east, where cascades fell
    and strove to rise again, it wore a crown
        of clouds. You tasted seven kinds of rain,

sucked the vein of liquorous palm, hoisted a nauseous
    cup at Pakanbaru springs: Brimstone Toddy,
        Harrowgate Hell. To keep it down,

the sulfurous mess, a chaser of arrack.
    Now and again, to the monsoon's whine,
        that blessed compote, tambaku and hemp

puffed through a water pipe Malays called
    ganga bang, in India, a *bong*.
        Marsden, some wet hours slid

from the pages of your *History*, some
    went up in smoke.

vii. 'La-uddin

Kiria Minjan—The Scorpion.
In youth, left for dead on the scree (scampering
Abung, morning fire), a royal beak bent low to him,
a wide, covering wing.

It is the scorpion's nature,
as the proverb says, to sting; and so he did, the royal breast
he owed his life—*each soul, the hostage of his deeds*—
and filled his fist

with Cochin sapphires
from the cask of Ratu Bagus Buang. Fitted out
in Ratu's panchalangs, he plied his errand to Samangka,
where sea-cows feast on melon.

From spies, Nakhoda Muda
learned Ratu's plan: take one hundred captive in the barks,
parade the shamed Malays before Rejangs in sooty villages,
seduce them all with vows

to snap Batavia's stalk.
A Council called by night: Nakhoda Muda plied the drowsy pangerans
with promises, begged them to keep faith with the Sultan and the Dutch;
Wasub was sent, his son

and emissary, with pepper,
oaths, and tidings to Batavia where in the lodge of Mynheer Sambirik
he met a foundling from Utrecht, indentured
to the Company.

In Tino's sharkfin eyes
rocked twenty weeks of waves, his mind tossed
beyond sleep. Like stranded fish, on braided mats they lay,
while Tino told his tales:

Epiphany, I clanged the frozen bells
from tower to turret, and clanged again, when suddenly,
Hoogstraaten kirk took wing, and up we flew

above the hills of Holland
fields lay like Turkey carpets
frozen lakes made O's

with silver mouths
saints from their portals turned the fields
to angelbroed, red tulips gaped

in snow. Skating children heard
a crack deep as the earth,
and all at once they sank

into the black heart of the mere.
Which saint took all the babes?
the grieving mothers asked, the Father

or the Son? And once the kirk touched down
I never saw one step inside again,
nor heard a blessing

pass their unkissed lips.
Wasub whispered, *another.*
In a soft cheek, the bone worked.

162

viii. Marsden

Our recreations, mainly backgammon,
and Irish, the occasional round of euchre.
Rabok, our servingboy, prepared a deck
stripped of underlings; all rank,
no file. Sundays we read Psalms
or Lamentations, a brace of Scottish
hymns in deference to our Primo,
MacLachan. The hour passed slowly
in pews hand-hewn from mahogany,
carven grapes and chalices
hard on our backs.
                              The rains came gentle on,
a morning sprinkle, dusky shower;
then jackal-crazy gusts. A great hand
spread its fingers over us, not a shutter
stayed in place. The downpour
seemed to course inside us till
we took it for the beating of our blood.

'Twas then Necessity, great mother
of et cetera unwombed the Fort Marlborough
Shakespeare Troupe, not, as widely rumoured,
I. Our debut, *The Winter's Tale, Or*
A Congelation Devoutly to be Wish'd.
To Moore I gave Leontes's role, and took
Polixenes myself; to Rotherhithe,
of open brow and decent mien, Camillo;
the rogue Autolychus went straight
to glowering Douglass of Strathclyde.

ix.

Hermione, she of *pinching fingers, paddled palms,*
  whose life stood in the level of his dreams?
    Who, *innocence for innocence,* inhaled

the air of sixteen years as in a single
  breath and let it out before the world's eyes?
    To him you taught your mother tongue, who took

between his lips and flawless teeth
  a line from Milton or a verse from Pope,
    and left it smoked in jaggri bark, kissed

with a scent of pergularia,
  all consonants, all rhymes dissolved
    in fluent hisses of the surf. Seven

years astride a teakwood bench
  as monsoons whined and waned, words tossed
    between you like a java-rubber ball,

Malay to English, English to Malay,
  all for your dictionary's sake. He never lived
    to see the book. Between its covers, cordovanned

and gilt, emboldened words like sentries ranged
  at intervals upon a ridge, between
    these sheets, the impress of his heart and soul,

faint as a watermark. Hermione
  went to good Wasub.

x. 'La-uddin

Nights on end, in Sambirik's lodge
the hurricano lantern burned. Stars sank their weary heads
on shouldered clouds. Wasub, Wasub
recall the verse:

the dog pants if you chase it away,
and pants if you leave it alone. He thought he saw his mother's hair
dance in the flames, his father's sampans bob upon Samangka's waves,
as Tino's voice, slight as a girl's,

ravelled all ends to beginnings.

No sooner had they crossed
the Oosterscheide
than it began to swell and flooded

all the plains from Roosendaal to Zeist,
herring trapped in branches,
briny fruit. This was no ordinary sea,

but a vat of tears
cried by the Wolf-Queen, mourning
her torn Wolf-Prince.

Nakhoda Muda waited for Wasub. By day,
beneath the latticed shadows of a chinkareen, he scanned the waves; by night,
amid the keening waves, the stars. And when a new moon
whelped a squall

the sea's great mouth swallowed
sampans of plantains, broke ribs of panchalangs upon its back.
He knew the time had come to leave seafaring to his sons.
Sambirik was pitiless,

intent upon his meerschaum
and his concubine, but before a new moon rose again,
Bantam sent pitch-and-timbered sloops bearing
a title: *Kei Damang*.

And we paid homage to Bantam,
passed beneath the silken canopies where eunuchs burnished
silver betel-stands. *Does man think we shall never put his bones
together again? who draws out tiny fingers?*

and at the Sultan's knees,
my father bowed his head, renounced the boat, so as to keep his sons
from debt. The royal name, the title Allah destined
for his bones, that he prayed to take

into gardens watered by running streams,
he kept. Now he was Kei Damang.
Now Kei Damang was he.

xi. Marsden

A brief digression on the Rejang tribe:

They have no God. Their *dewas*
(*deus* bastardized) lurk
about ancestral graves, nameless
household godlings; and bound by equal parts
of apprehension and affection, Rejangs drink
only from wells of the dead; the hills
they cut their teeth on take them, toothless, in.
Had they a god, he'd wear a tiger's face;
he's *nenek*, ancestor, and not *machang*
(and never mind his taste for human blood).
They say he reigns in palaces of bone
thatched with women's hair. By night
(if Shanklin—or his whiskey—may be trusted)
they crouch beside the hogfoot-baited traps
set by the Company to save their necks
and when the beast approaches, whisper *nenek
mattoi, mattoi!—careful, death is near!*
lest his blood be on their hands.

Rejangs.

                The Battaak
tell how earth began: Princess Puti-orla
rode a white owl out of heaven: fearful
for his daughter's life, King Batara
visited his mother in the sea—
a brew of mud and flame, such was the milk

he drew from her both her teats; and thence he formed
the flaming ramparts of the world.
'Tis true, what has been said of the Battaak
(*vide* Di Conti, De Barbosa, Beaulieu):
they do eat human flesh, but as a mode
of shewing detestation of a crime; in the event,
the local *raja* must assent, dispatch
a square of cloth to cover the offender's face,
together with a dish of salt and lemon.

xii.

A Malay meets Allah everywhere:
  pillowed on his mother's thighs
      in the ragged seam between his wife's—

so said Wasub. Strange that a man of forfeitures
  and resignations (unwived, not wifeless;
      not childless, unfathering) should put it thus.

Well, Ramadan had left him parched and weak.
  And when the weary
      sun laid down his sack to sprawl

upon a barrowcloud, when palsied scriveners
  and junior clerks slept babu-style beneath
      the breadfruit trees, when heat-lashed shade

outhushed the heat—
  then you rehearsed your play.

xiii. 'La-uddin

As children loosen *mampalams*
with thumbnails, young men take a blade to *jacca* fruit.
I taught him how, the son of Captain Poer; he wore his parents like a hat,
his father's flaring ears, his mother's

bleachèd hair, but somehow dodged his temper
and her squint. Samangka's children feared him, as we feared Captain Poer.
Unasked, my father built them a henhouse and a pigeoncote;
they added rawcord fences

and a sty, then cleared
our pepper plants from view. There, servants nailed themselves a hut.
They called our sweet Samangka (where melons give up sugar
to the sea), *Poerdorp.*

And how they came to be among us?
May the prophet and angels assist me.

Some say the Fiscal,
jealous of Damang, put forth a rumour—forbidden trade with Englishmen
had been resumed at Kei's command. Some said
it was a Tappanouli Corsican

one of d'Estaing's marauders,
who ran a Frenchmen's brothel in Bantam. Who knows the truth?
Trust ran aground between Samangka and Batavia.
To make amends,

my father paid Sambirik's fine
and for his pains, was taken prisoner by Captain Poer;
the Sultan, busy with his cockfights, let it pass.
And so they came,

my father's captor, Poer,
his wife and son and servantboy: a grey-eyed slender stalk of chaff,
a crumb of Dutch cheese.

The next tide brought Wasub.

xiv. Marsden

Such bickering, and such ineptitude!
Our Wicklow pantomime outShakespear'd this.
As Leontes, Douglass snorted, growled
and stamped, like a Sicilian buffalo;
and Rotherhithe, who looked a fine, if musclebound
Camillo, could not raise his voice above
a moth's.
                        But *mirabile dictu*, by torchlight
in Bencoolen Hall, before a hundred souls
the centre held:
                        Wasub played Hermione
to my adroit Polixenes, with all the grace
and bearing of a Queen
whose tender cadences pulled like the surf
at our astonished hearts, her *verily*—
indeed—*as potent as a lord's*.
Met with such grace of execution,
such demure and (dare I say it) womanly
aplomb as one would seek in vain at Vauxhall
or Tonbridge—I outdid myself.
When faint Camillo mumbled his *forbiddenly*,
I filled the air with rage and oaths, as if
my blue Bohemian blood had turned
infected jelly, my sterling reputation
to a reek. Indeed, MacLachan said
*my hideous savour struck the dullest nostril
in the crowd.*

And in the role of Time
I made my mark as well, begged reprieve
for *my swift passage o'er sixteen years*
with nimble capers and beguiling leaps;
and so persuasive was my mimic gaze
into a vapourous glass, they craned their necks.

Truly, *I gave my scene such growing*
as they had slept between.

XV.

And if *a sad tale's best*
   for winter, as your bard and namesake said,
      November gives you pause to watch the moorhens

knead the oaten skies of Hertfordshire
   to roost, before another month is out,
      beneath Sardinian eaves.

xvi. 'La-uddin

May Allah raze them
from the earth, Batavia, Muara Tanda, Poerdorp
and leave it scored and pitted where they lay.
On the Day of Days

men shall become
like scattered moths; the mountains, tufts of carded wool.
May those betrayed be succoured at the quinine springs
of Salsabil, which healed

the Prophet's pilgrim foot.

For years I kept this tale between my teeth for Wasub's sake,
how he tumbled out of time, as will the firedancing souls
who forget God made them

from bloody clumps of flesh,
who do not reflect on the camels, who heed the mischief of the slinking
prompter, *did he make you? You?*

how he pinned the doorway shut
with sago twigs lest a child watering the earth between her heels
might see a roil of arms and legs, unwombèd twins
aspill upon the ground,

mouth pressed to mouth,
as though the aching breath of life could be forsworn, the lamp
threw shadows of a giant cockchafer, upon the thatch
beneath the writhing stars

it heaved and twitched
in rhythms of its own, and *tinka, tinka, tinka* went its song. . .

At Captain Poer's request,
Kei Damang and his sons followed in a praw
to pay a visit on Nakhodas at Croee. At Muara Tanda, wordlessly,
the Hollanders put in their ketch,

and burned MacLachan's lemon orchard
to the ground; a jagged line of stakes thrown on the dirt
unpinned a patch of England from the earth,
smoke took its ashen tale upwind.

They said, a glass of arrack
on the Captain's deck, *opla!*—boats winked together and apart.
And as we boarded, Kei Damang and both his sons,
they drew our krisses from us,

bound our hands,
and took us prisoner. Then Tino spat and went below.

xvii. Marsden

Our carver's excellence, indeed; Wasub
came honestly by wrinkles on his brow,
years of squinting in the sun.
Just as they never say their names, Malays,
they never tell their age, and truth be told
it wasn't clear he knew. I guessed he had
a dozen years on me, but then they age
with an alacrity untypical
of Englishmen.
               Which is to say
he looked the part: rice flour dusted
cheeks and shoulder, betel streaked his mouth
(*the ruddiness upon her lips is wet*);
with linen fresh unmangled, warmth hid
in its folds, I draped him, head to foot.
The pose he struck was not as we'd rehearsed;
head cocked, eyes wider than the night
we bivouacked below the Lasa Hills
and saw orangutans put up their mocking palms
to fire; what *evils conjured to remembrance*
left Sicily appalled were nought to those
that struggled for a kind of life in Wasub's eyes
and made him, lost in weeping, theirs.
And when the cue came—*you perceive she stirs*—
he shivered visibly, whose ear had shaped
the words into a romance of his own,
so still, Leontes stepped upon the bamboo pedestal
and held a hundred souls within his profferred hand

and only buckled shadows and the cicadas' rasp
prevailed to eke flesh out of timeless stone.

He took Leontes' hand and came, still weeping, down.

177

xviii.

What plied between his Allah
  and himself? You were never wont
    to say—I doubt you knew—

nor *make it manifest where he has liv'd*
  or how stol'n from the dead.

xix. Marsden

                    Fifty years
have passed, and in Croee are some
who still say I played Time more grandly than
Bohemia; well, my temper's one part
philosophical, one part historical,
two parts dramatical. Besides, 'tis nature's
truth:
                    Hermione shan't be wooed.

I bowed, struck the scenery and doused
the tusser wicks, but never told the denouement.
And Allah, bless him, is as mum as I.

xx. 'La-uddin

Three days and nights we lay on deck
in Spanish irons, Tino's narrow eye above his pistolet's black mouth.
Given a rats' nest of rotting cord, we plaited lines,
the sea's fist pounded out the hours.

And when they slew our buffalo,
the stink of roasted flesh rose from their terrible bimbangs,
the bones they hurled to sea
Samangka carried back to shore

on grieving waves.
I prayed *O break their skin with teeth, their teeth*
on bones, their bones on rocks, my father's head bowed
in prayers of his own

while Dutchmen spooned a pot
of layang-layang soup, Wasub stood in his irons, licked
his cracked and bloody lips and dived
between the parted fingers of the sea

xxi.

This little I know:
  In the tin dish by his hammock,
     Wasub concocted

rosemary and rue: a paste
  of sago bark and orpiment, the first,
     to dull his senses; the last to stop his heart

at which it failed. A week
  he teetered on oblivion;
     in lieu of physic or physician,

Chalmers' mumbled, Presbyterian
  —*pray for his soul*—your midnights,
     Marsden, and your noons.

Though not a pious man, you said
  a blessing on his prostrate soul,
     the heavy hours lay like guineas

on his heart. Afterwards
  you never spoke of it, recovery
     adequate to bring the dictionary

to an end. He'd changed, his eyes
  wandered from the page,
     an inattentive child

following a file of ants,
  he scanned the ferns
     for phrases once his own.

xxii. 'La-uddin

Praise Allah, then we ran amok

a savage clamour in the bow,
my father's dagger-bitten
flesh, Tino's elbow

cambered like a willow
on a lacquer box
bending, lifting, bending

Kei Damang's blood
slow to depart,
red streams down his arm, black pond at his feet

and Tino's spattered
scarlet pinfeathers
on my two hands.

The boom of English canon
splintered Dutch masts, cracked ribs
of boats and men alike

and when I dived,
flesh bobbed for cormorants,
sank for sharks.

At Bencoolen they said
an English yawl en route
to view the scorchèd groves at Muara Tanda,

had pulled my brother from the sea,
laid him on deck. My mind's blade
peels back rumour's skin—

a chamois cloth
moistened with palm oil,
a level hand that swabbed

my brother's flaming face
the face he opened eyes on
dim and kind,

mouth rounding words
he'd find his own
lips make

in days to come.

xxiii. Marsden

                        Fishing hookless
like the Achinese, we felt among
the roots for carp, who *tuba*-dreamed
their way into our hands. Next, I thought,
a gazetteer of coastal islands;
Engano, Sanding, Pulo Triste, perhaps
a study of Japan; "next, *next*;" my voice
ran down his neck like summer rain.
From time to time, he told an old, cracked
Holland tale of wings and wolves. And thus
his mind's eye rounded the earth

until an early autumn fever brought
his glossary of heartache to an end.

xxiv. 'La-uddin

The next Indiaman to sway
out of Bencoolen harbor, bound for Good Hope,
St. Helena and Plymouth, had me for freight.
When the Flood rose high

we carried you in the floating ark.

So ends the tale of Kei Damang, commissioned
by the Cardiff Orientalist Society, recorded by
his eldest son, at Bantam House, Royal Crescent, Bath

who never saw his father
and his brother into Allah's earth, but left
them bathed where waves lick clean the melon seeds
on Samangka's shores.

XXV.

In Nelson's wake, you rose to eminence.
　　As Secretary of the Admiralty, you took
　　　　the one-armed hero's obsequies

to your sole charge, raven crepe
　　upon the stallions' skirts, gilded bosses
　　　　on the catafalque. They said a baronetcy

lay in your neighbourhood,
　　and they were wrong.
　　　　Did bitterness or generosity

cede your pension to the crown?—
　　for which the Parliamentary applause
　　　　carried to Hertfordshire.

xxvi. Marsden

         The spines of all my books
are gilt: my *History of Sumatra,*
Corrected and Improved, flanked by
translations into German, French, and Dutch;
my catalogue of Oriental coins,
Marco Polo Englished; and a teakwood
bookstand built to order by a Punjab
joiner down in Potter's Bar, bearing
Marsden's Dictionary of Malay

in which, from time to time, I peer
as in glass and see, or think I see,
a face nor wholly mine, nor his,
but catching something of us both,
as though there passed between us
not eight years, but one word,
partly a query, partly an answer.

(*All for my dictionary's sake.*)

            This evening,
phantoms quicken in the library:
McMahon and Moriat, my Celtic
tragedy, stunted at Act Three,
a dozen brief Anacreontic odes
scribbled while he dozed, the *Coastal Gazetteer,*
barely begun; unpublished tracts
delivered to the Royal Society,
Beliefs and Customs of the Battaak Tribe.

And my *Comparative Analphabetic Guide*
to Five East Indian Tongues with Sanskrit
and Kashmirian Synonimaes?
It languishes, since my catastrophe—
thrown from a mare, sprawled in the Bushey Road;
I have attained an age, as Graham was wont to say,
when illness never leaves us where it finds us.

This has indeed become a winter's tale.

In March, a touch of apoplexy left me
some degrees remote from where I was;
my left hand's uncorrected, unimproved
my right, a widow pacing back and forth
upon a narrow pier, to catch a glimpse of sail
before it goes. I keep a spaniel, Raffles,
with me on my walks, and when it rains
I feed him points of toast with muscat jam,
a practice common in some parts of Wales.

Biographical Note

ESTHER SCHOR, a poet and professor of English at Princeton University, won the National Jewish Book Award for *Emma Lazarus*. A specialist in British Romanticism, her scholarship includes *Bearing the Dead: The British Culture of Mourning from the Enlightenment to Victoria* and *The Cambridge Companion to Mary Shelley*. She is soon to complete a book on the past and present of the Esperanto movement, forthcoming from Metropolitan Books. Her essays and reviews have appeared in *The New York Times Book Review*, *The New Republic*, *The Times Literary Supplement*, *Raritan* and *The Forward*. She lives in Princeton, New Jersey.

NOTES for *Strange Nursery*

For encouragement and support, I'm indebted to Walter Greenblatt, with thanks also to Graham Burnett, Maayan Dauber, Maria DiBattista, Jeff Dolven, Anne Barrett Doyle, Michael Greenberg, Langdon Hammer, J. D. McClatchy, Paul Muldoon, Deborah Nord, James Richardson, Jonathan Rosen, Ivy Baer Sherman, Willard Spiegelman, Susan Stewart, and Jonathan Wilson. Thanks to Dean Drummond for a tour of the Harry Partch instruments and for his companionship.

Stanley Moss's love for poems and animals are an ongoing inspiration.

Much of the travel that gave rise to these poems was supported by the Office of the Dean of the Faculty, Princeton University. I am grateful also to the Princeton faculty and staff who have taught me what I know about the care and use of animals in research.

Cover image attributed to Maerten de Vos

Aplomado Falcon photo courtesy of Rosamund Purcell

Harvest: This poem is about how we press knowledge out of living things; how we decide whether knowledge of life is or is not worth its cost in life.

For two years, I served as a non-scientist member of a university Institutional Animal Care and Use Committee (IACUC). The Committee vets all research protocols involving animals to ensure that procedures cause a minimum of pain and use the minimum number of appropriate animals. It also inspects the vivarium—the "strange nursery" that houses the animals—twice yearly.

Before being appointed, I was asked if I had any objection in principle to animal experimentation. I said I did not. As a child, I had visited lab animals in my father's pharmaceutical firm; as an adult, I watched my parents (one with cancer, one with Alzheimer's) benefit from drugs developed through animal testing. I know that I may one day benefit from the same drugs, or others.

I received no formal training (though on-line tutorials were offered later), and had to rely on the good will and advice of my colleagues in Psychology, Molecular Biology, and Ecology and Evolutionary Biology; of the vivarium staff; and of the university veterinarian. Their work requires them to balance empathy for animals with the need to know more about life, its diseases, and its remedies. This is not an easy task, and it was a privilege to work with them.

At the same time that I was learning to read protocols, I was studying Tractate Sotah of the Talmud. Here I discovered an ancient protocol for acquiring knowledge, in this case, the "knowledge" of whether a woman suspected of adultery was guilty or not. And here were the Rabbis offering commentaries and guidance, as my colleagues had done.

The left-hand side of the poem contains quotations from these protocols, modern and ancient, scientific and religious; on the right appears guidance and commentary, both of my scientific colleagues and of the rabbis. And from my two years of immersion in the world of ethical animal research, in which I, too, had to decide whether knowledge of life is or is not worth its cost in life, emerged the italicized text in the center of the page.

Budapest

I Szigetvár: *Zrínyi's Charge from the Fortress of Szigetvar*, by Johann Peter Krafft (1825), Hungarian National Museum. In 1566, during the siege of Szigetvár, the corpse of Suleiman the Magnificent was presented in battle against the Habsburgs, led by the poet-warrior Miklos Zrínyi; as at the Battle of Mohács, the Ottomans prevailed.
II Aszú: A sweet wine from the Tokaj region of Hungary, it ferments for at least seven years in the vat.
VI Radnoti's Pocket: Hungarian Jewish poet Miklos Radnoti (1909-1944) was shot by the Nazis and buried in a mass grave. Eighteen months later he was exhumed; in his pocket was found a notebook with his final lyrics.

Ulica Okolnik 2: The address of the Warsaw Conservatory. Umschlagplatz, a railroad siding adjacent to the Warsaw Ghetto created by the Nazis in 1942 for deporting Jews to Treblinka.

Bread of the Sun

"Life is never truly ours, it always belongs to the others,
life is no one's, we all are life—
bread of the sun for the others,
the others that we all are –"
    Octavio Paz, *Piedra de Sol*, tr. Eliot Weinberger

II Zona Rosa: a neighborhood of nightclubs in Mexico City.
III Pirates: Chapultepec, a large public park in Mexico City.
IV At Monte Albán: A pre-Columbian archeological site in Oaxaca, Mexico. The anthropologist Paul Kirchhoff (1900-1972), a Jewish refugee from Hitler's Germany, was nearly deported to Germany in 1936 when his American visa was not renewed. Thanks to funds supplied by anthropologist Melville Herskovits, Kirchhoff decamped to Mexico, where he and the *Grupo de Trabajadores Marxistas* demanded that the workers of

Spain break with socialists, Stalinists, and anarchists in order to constitute a "Soviet Spain." See Chapter 5, "The War in Spain," in Philippe Bourrinet, *The "Bordigist" Current 1919-1999* http://www.left-dis.nl.

Achilles at Dien Bien Phu: Trained at Saumur, the elite cavalry academy, and a record-setting jumper, Col. (later Brigadier General) Christian de la Croix de Castries (1902-1991), held out for fifty-five days at Dien Bien Phu against the guerrilla warfare of the Viet Minh. De Castries' surrender to General Vo Nguyen Giap on May 17, 1953 brought the French presence in Indochina to an end. French officers wept when captured, but de Castries' reading of the *Iliad* is fiction. Crécy, key battle of the Hundred Years' War (1346) in which the force of English longbows vanquished heavily armored French soldiers under Phillip VI. Oran, Algerian region where de Castries was taken prisoner by the Germans.

Sapere Vedere: In memory of Jean Ciardiello.

La Rambla: In memory of the poet Saul Bennett. Pedestrian thoroughfare and pet market in Barcelona.

Guide for the Perplexed: Based loosely on Maimonides' discussion of the negative attributes of God.

For Lori: An acrostic for Lori Schor.

Hearsay: Epigraph from *On Marvellous Things Heard* [pseudo-Aristotle], Trans W. S. Hett. London: Heinemann, 1955.

Strange Nursery: For Margie Barrett.

NOTES for *The Hills of Holland*

Guggenheim Abstract: *Millecentonovantasei*, 1996. The poem followed a visit to "Abstraction in the Twentieth Century: Total Risk, Freedom, Discipline" at the Solomon R. Guggenheim Museum, 1996.

Opera Without Words: *get*: a writ of divorce; *sheytlmacher*: a wig-maker.

Cumbria: With the exception of "Edinburgh: The Scottish National War Memorial," all poems refer to sites and topographical features in the county of Cumbria in the Lake District of England.
   At Dove Cottage: Helen Darbishire (1881-1961), co-editor (with Ernest de Selincourt) of *The Poetical Works of William Wordsworth* (Oxford University Press, 1940-49), is said to have initiated the microfilming of the Dove Cottage archives immediately after the bombing of Hiroshima. The story is probably apocryphal.

Alef: brucha, a blessing.

The Hills of Holland: The poem is an historical fiction; very historical and very fictive. It comprises three strands. The first is a narrative by the orientalist and linguist William Marsden, written in Hertfordshire in 1835, the year before his death. Marsden's story recalls his time in the British colony at Bencoolen (now Bengkulu), Sumatra, during which he collaborated on a Malay-English dictionary with Wasub, whom he had rescued from the sea. The story leading up to Wasub's rescue—a story Marsden does not know; the tale of Wasub's betrayal by his lover, a Dutch sailor named Tino—is told in a courtly poem of 1829 by his brother, Nakhoda 'La-uddin, a Malay immigrant living in Bath. The rest—that is, the third strand of unattributed sections –is commentary, but the midrashic kind, which ventures to fill in some gaps.
   In fact, the historical Marsden translated the historical 'La-uddin's, *Memoirs of a Malayan Family, Written by Themselves,* trans. W. Marsden (London, 1830), but the narratives of Wasub and Tino, and of Marsden and Wasub, are entirely fictional.
   Aside from the narrative of 'La-uddin, I have also drawn on William Marsden's great *History of Sumatra* (London, 1811) and the entry on Marsden in the *Dictionary of National Biography*. Quotations from *The Koran* are drawn from N. J. Dawood, ed., *The Koran* (Penguin, 1997); quotations from *The Winter's Tale*, from G. Blakemore Evans, et al, eds., *The Riverside Shakespeare* (Houghton Mifflin, 1974).